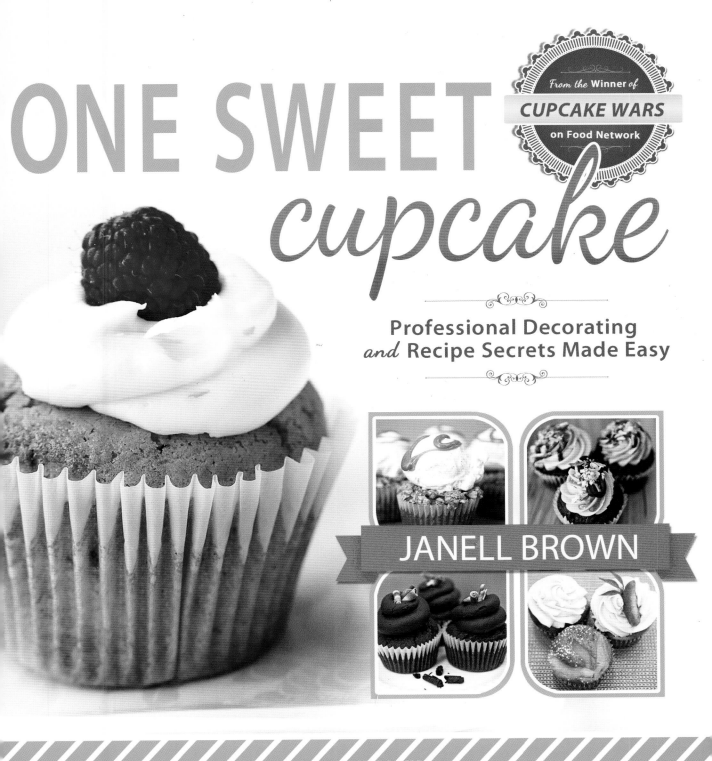

ONE SWEET *cupcake*

From the Winner of
CUPCAKE WARS
on Food Network

Professional Decorating
and Recipe Secrets Made Easy

JANELL BROWN

FRONT TABLE BOOKS
AN IMPRINT OF CEDAR FORT, INC. | SPRINGVILLE, UTAH

ISBN 13: 978-1-4621-1235-7

Published by Front Table Books, an imprint of Cedar Fort, Inc.
2373 W. 700 S., Springville, UT 84663
Distributed by Cedar Fort, Inc., www.cedarfort.com

Library of Congress Cataloging-in-Publication Data

Brown, Janell, 1979-
  One sweet cupcake / Janell Brown.
    pages cm
  Includes index.
  ISBN 978-1-4621-1235-7 (hardcover)
  1. Cupcakes. I. Title.
  TX771.B8767 2013
  641.8'653--dc23
                          2013018609

Cover and page design by Erica Dixon
Cover design © 2013 by Lyle Mortimer
Edited by Casey J. Winters

Printed in China

10 9 8 7 6 5 4 3 2 1

Praise For ONE SWEET cupcake

"A divine book full of fabulous cupcake and icing recipes that will make your mouth water! I'm heading to the kitchen right now to use some of Janell's succulent recipes and amazing tips and secrets!"

Kara Allen
The "New" Martha Stewart;
Author of *Kara's Party Ideas*

"*One Sweet Cupcake* is a visibly delicious cookbook that will appeal to cupcake fans everywhere. There seems to be a never-ending rainbow of recipes that could turn even the most casual baker into a serial cupcake manufacturer. Janell gives you everything you need to make your cupcakes not just perfect, but perfectly beautiful. Recipes are easy to read, instructions easy to follow, and the book dangerous to peruse. . . . I will definitely be purchasing multiple copies to give out this Christmas, because everyone could use *One Sweet Cupcake* to get them through the holidays, and every day!"

Melissa Richardson
Coauthor of *The Art of Baking
with Natural Yeast*

"*One Sweet Cupcake* is more than just a fabulous cookbook from Janell Brown, creator of the award-winning bakery One Sweet Slice. For people like me who need easy step-by-step baking instructions, these are wonderful recipes for creating delicious and beautiful cupcakes for any occasion that bring a bit of delightful goodness into your home."

H.B. Moore
Best of State and
Whitney Award–Winning Author

"I didn't mean to become such a die-hard cupcake fan! But my daughters and I started making One Sweet Slice part of our Saturday routine during the farmer's market, and now I'm hooked. What amazes me is that everything is always perfect! I consider myself a pretty great hobby-baker, so I usually don't buy things that I know I could do better. Janell outdoes herself with every recipe!"

Debbie Worthen
TV Host, KUTV Channel 2

"I love to stop by One Sweet Slice for my sweet tooth indulgence, but now I can make all of Janell's great flavors right in my home! One of the best cupcake books on the market to make champion bakers out of everyone!"

Mary Crafts-Homer
CEO/President, Culinary Crafts;
Winner of the International Caterer of the Year
by the International Caterers Association

"As a mother of five daughters, we are always in the kitchen. We have tried just about every cupcake from Los Angeles to New York City, and nothing beats One Sweet Slice. We can't wait to experience the fun of creating our own sweet slices at home!"

Christena Huntsman Durham
Huntsman Foundation Board

"Janell has been delighting brides at the Canyons Resort for several years with her inspirational designs and absolutely delicious cakes. She offers an extensive list of flavors that could appease even the most discerning person. . . . Her talent seems to have no boundaries."

Brooke Hafets
Director of Food & Beverage Events and Sales,
Canyons Resort

Breyn McCormick
Catering Services Manager,
Canyons Resort

"Beyond making the most delicious baked goods I have ever had, Janell is the most creative designer of cakes and treats I have ever met. They are magical. One Sweet Slice is my go-to spot for my celebrity events and parties."

Lisa Barlow
CEO, Luxe Marketing; President, Vida Tequila

"A beautiful and yummy documentation of an inspiring dream come to life. Janell has presented her fans with a huge collection of recipes that truly represent her and One Sweet Slice and the delicious success that it is!"

Lindi Haws
Love-The-Day.com Blog Founder
and Party Stylist

"Janell is a complete joy to work with! I love how she brings my clients' visions to life with her edible creations. No matter how unique or creative a request may be, Janell and the staff of One Sweet Slice always deliver an impeccable product and amazing customer service. As an event planner, my mind is put to ease whenever I work with Janell. Her attention to detail and her organization skills when it comes to providing for my clients [are] unmatched. For these reasons and many more, I continue to recommend One Sweet Slice."

Michelle Cousins
Utah Events by Design

CONTENTS

Classics

Sweet & Light

The Dark Side

Warm & Comforting

A Little Nutty

Icings

Toppings & Fillings

Easy Decorating Ideas

Preface

I did not grow up dreaming to one day own a bakery. I do not have a grandmother who loves to bake and has passed her recipes down to each of her grandchildren, and my first memories are not of my mother baking in the kitchen. I did have an appreciation for delicious baked goods when I was a child—what child doesn't?—and my favorite dessert was a warm gooey brownie with a cold glass of milk. My discovery of baking was unplanned and came later in life.

At age ten I picked up a few bottles of acrylic paint from my mother's stash and started to repaint my bedroom. My favorite part of my science fair projects was decorating the board, and I enjoyed trying to make our Sunday box mix cakes look like something from a Betty Crocker magazine—I love being creative, working with what I have, making things that taste amazing and look beautiful, and finding a good challenge.

At age twenty-five I had just received my bachelor's degree in interpersonal communications

and was expecting the birth of our first son. One month later I started to take cake decorating classes at a local craft store, to develop a new hobby and give myself a night out each week. I quickly fell in love with the creative outlet cake decorating provided, and the idea of using sugar as an art medium was incredible. Art you could eat! After completing the three-month course, I began assisting my instructor and taught basic cake decorating classes for two years. Making cakes became my favorite pastime, and I filled my weekends with orders for family and friends. During this time I was expecting our third baby. After her birth, I decided to quit teaching and start a small cake decorating business at home.

The state of Utah allows people to run licensed kitchens from their homes. After completing tedious paperwork, having my home inspected, and explaining to my children that after eight o'clock the kitchen was closed, I set up shop. I began by posting an ad in the local classified section of one of Salt Lake's online newspapers.

With a few unprofessional pictures and a discounted price of one hundred dollars for a three-tiered wedding cake, I offered my services as a cake decorator. By the end of the first month I had five wedding cakes booked and had even charged one bride the staggering price of two hundred dollars! I had three small children under the age of three, so all of my baking and decorating had to be done at night, after they had gone to bed. I spent many late nights mixing, baking, icing, and decorating. I became a night owl and looked forward to the long hours of listening to my old high school music and talking with my husband, Trent, while I worked. It was during one of these conversations that the name "One Sweet Slice" evolved. The name was selected because, first, the website address was available and, second, I felt it represented what I was trying to do. I was creating cakes that would help celebrate some of the sweetest moments in life! Events that were a slice out of the ordinary. Trent set up a small website, and he began to market our little business online. Word of mouth began to spread, and requests started to pour in.

For six years, I balanced my love of cake decorating, my love for my family, and everything that comes with a fast-paced, young, always a little chaotic, and slightly messy household. Trent supported me in every way possible. Often I would find him letting me sleep in, fixing dinner, playing with neglected children, kneading fondant, and delivering cakes. When I became overtired or discouraged, instead of telling me to quit, he would offer suggestions or look for ways he could help. He was the only one who consistently saw how much work went on behind the scenes and understood and supported my crazy desire to keep baking and cake decorating a part of my life.

In December 2010, three days after Christmas, opportunity knocked. My husband had been laid off from work. I was six weeks away from delivering our fourth child and was looking forward to having a few months to relax and focus on my new baby. Little did I know the next few months would be full of stress, major decisions, sleepless nights, and life-changing events! Always an entrepreneur at heart, Trent expressed the desire to start his own business, and after looking at our options, we decided to join forces. We made the decision to open our shop while I was in the hospital with our new baby! Four months and a ridiculous amount of work later, we opened the doors of One Sweet Slice Custom Cake & Cupcake Shoppe.

During our first year we won multiple awards, including Best Cupcakes and Best Wedding Cakes for 2011 in the Salt Lake area. We were named South Jordan's Small Business of the Year in 2012, and in 2013 we won *City Weekly's* Best of Utah and the prestigious Best of State. We have been featured in local, national, and international bridal magazines, including *Utah Bride & Groom, Park City Bride & Groom, Zions Bank Community*, and *Utah Business*. We have appeared on *Good Things Utah*, KSL's *Studio 5*, and Channel 2's *Fresh from the Kitchen*. In September 2011, we competed on Food Network's

Cupcake Wars and won! Being asked to compete on Food Network was a chance of a lifetime. My good friend and pastry extraordinaire Kristen Cold competed with me on the Star Wars challenge. It was incredible to see the amount of work and talent the producers and competitors put into each episode. The thrill of winning a televised national competition and ten thousand dollars is something I'll never forget!

Winning *Cupcake Wars* has opened countless doors of opportunity and has changed our lives. We now have a second location and continue to look for ways to share our passion for cake with everyone.

My hope in writing this book is to share what I love and what I have learned about the art of baking a beautiful and delicious cupcake.

Acknowledgments

My first and biggest thank you goes to my Father in Heaven for giving me and my husband, Trent, so much challenge and opportunity. It has been amazing to see the change in each of us. The growth we've had has been a hard but great experience. Without Trent, this book wouldn't be here and the doors to our shops would be closed! He holds everything together, gives it direction, and makes it run. My understanding, appreciation, and love for him has grown immensely in the past two years. I can't say thank you enough times. Our children (ages 9, 7, 5, and 2) have put up with the brunt of our crazy schedules, my cranky attitude when I've had no sleep, and the constant busyness and chaos of having two parents trying to learn how to run a business. They have been forgiving, loving, and patient as only children can. I can't express enough appreciation to our family, friends, and neighbors for their continued love and support. A continuing thank you to both of our parents. Their love, support, encouragement, and endless hours of babysitting have made all this possible. A huge thank you to Kristen for accepting the challenge to compete on *Cupcake Wars* with me! There would have been no victory without her cool head, great ideas, and the fastest chocolate cupcake wraps I have ever seen. Thank you to Dustin, Devin, and Tyler for all of their running around and last-minute help. Thank you to all of our staff at One Sweet Slice, especially Melanie, Annelise, and Ti for holding the fort down and putting up with my inconsistent schedule (or lack thereof) while I've been away and trying to get this book and five hundred other things finished! Thank you to Pepper Nix for teaching me the importance of a beautiful picture and all of the good times and great photos because of it. Thank you to Jen for her incredibly good eye, amazing pictures, and being able to take on more cupcakes than she can eat. Thank you Joanna Barker and Cedar Fort Publishing for asking me to put this together and being patient with me, my schedule, and my naïveté in writing a book. And finally a heartfelt thank you to our business advisors (Dan, Kathy, and Josh) for not giving up on us and being there with a knowing smile and comforting hug while listening to our triumphs and woes of running and growing a small business.

The Right Ingredients

One purpose in writing this book was to create a collection of recipes that are delicious, unique, easy to follow, and that could be made with accessible and recognizable ingredients.

There is nothing more frustrating than getting halfway through a recipe and discovering that you don't have one of the ingredients or, even worse, that you've never heard of it and have no idea where to buy it! This always seems to happen on a Sunday night—for some reason cupcakes always taste better on a Sunday night, and the last thing I want you to do is make a trip to the grocery store or send one of your kids to a neighbor's house asking for an ingredient that neither of you can pronounce (note: you can always blame the mispronunciation on your kids if needed).

These recipes are created with ingredients you can find at any local grocery store, and at least one out of five neighbors will have what you need if you don't already have it in your pantry. I grew up in a small town with one grocery store, and the closest Walmart was an hour away. Our "natural" food store was my mother's garden or my grandmother's five-year supply of canned fruit, fresh jams and preserves, hand-ground wheat, homemade yogurt, or warm cream scraped from the top of a pitcher of milk. Everything grown was used for cooking, for baking, or as a health remedy of some sort. The unspoken motto was, "Use what you have."

I believe in the importance of using the best ingredients that you have. The better your ingredients are, the better your end product will be. I also believe in practicality—it's not necessary to have organic farm eggs, or cocoa that costs a ridiculous amount of money and can only be found in a store you don't regularly shop at, to create an incredible-tasting cupcake. If you feel strongly about all-natural ingredients and shopping local, then purchase your ingredients from the shops you frequent. If you prefer the convenience and pricing of a box store, then purchase your ingredients there. Use the best you can!

Here are a few key ingredients that you will need to make sure you have on hand before you begin baking.

Wet

Butter: Unsalted butter is a must when baking. If at all possible, use only real butter and not margarine. Butter adds flavor and texture to your baking. The temperature of the butter is very important in baking. Always use room temperature butter, never cold. This allows the maximum amount of air to be beaten into your batter. Beating the butter first, before adding the other ingredients, will create air bubbles that the baking powder will enlarge during baking. Butter is essential for creating delicious icing, so do not substitute it.

Milk: The extra fat in whole milk adds another layer of flavor to your cupcakes and acts as a tenderizer and moisturizer. Your cake will have a more delicate crumb and will not be dry. In these recipes, the milk does not need to be at room temperature.

Buttermilk is the liquid left after butter is churned, and it creates a light tang in the taste of vanilla-based cakes. It is an acidic ingredient, like yogurt or sour cream, and helps tenderize the gluten in the batter and helps the cake to rise.

Eggs: Always use large eggs when baking. Eggs act as a leavening agent and add color, texture, flavor, and richness to the batter. They help to bind the other ingredients together. The air from beaten eggs acts as a leavening agent when it expands in the oven and causes the cake to rise. Eggs are also used to thicken custards, curds, and creams. The egg whites are used to make meringues. For these recipes, the eggs do not need to be at room temperature.

Sour cream: Sour cream is made from cultured cream. It acts as an emulsifier by holding the cake together and will give your cake a velvety texture. It has a high fat content and adds a rich flavor.

Vegetable oil: Canola oil is the ideal choice to use when baking. It is light, flavorless, and inexpensive. The oil acts as a bonding agent and is essential in adding moisture to the cake.

Fruit: Use fruit that is in season, is fresh, and, if possible, is organic.

Dry

Baking powder: Baking powder is a leavening agent that will cause batters to rise when baked. After the ingredients are creamed together, the leavener enlarges the air bubbles in the batter when the cupcakes are in the oven. Baking powder contains baking soda, cream of tartar, and cornstarch.

Salt: Salt is a flavor enhancer, and even though a small amount is used, it is crucial to baking! There are three different types of salt that can be used: iodized or table salt, kosher salt, and sea salt. If the salt has a fine grain, any of these three types can be used for baking.

Flour: Flour can be ground from a variety of nuts and seeds. These recipes call for wheat flour. Even among wheat flour there are many different types, and the type of flour used will ultimately affect the finished product. Because flour contains protein, it will produce gluten when it comes into contact with water and heat. The gluten gives elasticity and strength to baked goods. All-purpose flour is ideal for cupcakes and is used in each of these recipes

Sugar: Many types of sugars are available, but three are used in these recipes: granulated, brown, and powdered. Granulated sugar is produced from sugarcane or sugar beets and has been refined to small white granules. Brown sugar is refined white sugar with some of the molasses left in, which gives it a brown color. Powdered or confectioners' sugar is granulated sugar that has been ground to a powder and in which cornstarch has been added to reduce clumping and aid in thickening.

Sugar does more than simply sweeten cupcake batter. When sugar and butter are creamed together, the sugar granules rub against the fat in the butter and produce air bubbles. When the leavener is added, the gases enlarge the bubbles, causing the batter to rise when the cupcakes are placed in the oven. Sugar also has the ability to hold moisture, resulting in a tender cake crumb and a long shelf life. The sugar and butter in the batter is what causes cupcakes to brown during baking.

Chocolate: There are two types of unsweetened cocoa powder: Dutch processed or unsweetened. Dutch-processed cocoa is treated with an alkali to neutralize its acids. It has a reddish-brown color and light flavor, and it is easy to dissolve. Unsweetened cocoa is bitter and gives a deep, intense chocolate flavor.

Vanilla: This extract is used in every cupcake recipe and is extremely important. Pure vanilla extract, not vanilla flavoring, should be used. The extract comes from vanilla beans harvested in Central America and provides a rich and delicious flavor to each recipe. Infusing crushed vanilla beans into a sweet syrup creates vanilla bean paste. Using this paste in the recipe will leave small flecks of vanilla bean in the batter.

Baking Basics

Let's start at the beginning—it's a very good place to start, after all. The basics of baking involve good ingredients, proper equipment, and a great recipe. Make sure to buy the best ingredients that are available to you, and make sure you have all of the equipment you need before you begin. The equipment you use in baking is an investment; do it right.

Follow the steps in the order found in each recipe. There is science and reason to the purpose and order of each step.

Do not overmix your batter. A few minutes is all that is needed; any more will result in a hard, chewy, un-delicious cupcake.

Use fresh fruit whenever possible.

Use an oven thermometer, and don't forget to set the timer. It's always better to underbake and let the cupcakes bake for a little longer with your watchful eye than to overbake and end up with hard, dry cupcakes.

And finally, enjoy the process! Baking is about experimenting, learning, sharing, and taking part in a tradition and passion that has fueled the fire of creativity of bakers and decorators for hundreds of years and many more to come.

Essential Tools

The tools used in any trade are essential and make a difference in the quality of the work done. You will need to have a few important tools on hand before you begin the art of cupcake-making.

Muffin tins: Muffin tins come in all different shapes and sizes, from mini to jumbo.

Paper liners: Today, you can choose from many different types and sizes of cupcake liners. Colors can vary from white to hot-pink with polka dots. If you're using a patterned liner, use a vanilla-based cupcake so the pattern will still be visible when the cupcake is baked. Check the size of your liner before you start filling your cupcakes, and don't overfill or underfill them. Finally, think about how the liner you are using will affect the overall appearance and presentation of your cupcakes.

Ice cream scoop: A mechanical ice cream scoop is a great tool for filling cupcake liners with batter. It will make uniform scoops, which assists with even baking.

Toothpicks: Toothpicks are an easy way to determine if the center of a cupcake is done baking. When the toothpick is inserted into the center and comes out clean or with only a few crumbs, the cupcake is done. Most often I touch the top of the cupcake with my finger to ensure that the cupcake is completely done, but there are times when using a toothpick is best.

Cooling rack: As the name implies, a cooling rack is perfect for cooling baked goods, allowing the air to circulate quickly and evenly.

Oven thermometer: Oven temperatures vary and can be inaccurate. Using an oven thermometer allows you to monitor the true temperature of your oven and adjust it as needed.

Tools for Icing and Decorating

Pastry bag: A pastry bag is essential to icing uniformed cupcakes. It gives you control, keeps your hands clean, and will give your cupcakes a professional look. Disposable bags are easy to use, and they make the clean up simple.

Piping tips: To create the look of the cupcakes in this book, you will need a medium to large round tip and a medium to large star tip. Each brand of tip is numbered to make the ordering and replacement easier. We use Ateco numbers 848 and 809 the most. Like the name, the round tips create a clean, round edge while the star tip is beveled and creates raised edges on the icing.

Offset spatula: This is also known as an icing spatula. A small offset spatula is perfect for hand-icing cupcakes or for creating a rustic natural look for the top of your cupcakes.

Gel paste colors: More concentrated than liquid coloring, gel paste colors are the perfect choice for tinting icings and fondant. Only a few drops are generally needed, and they are available in a large variety of colors. They are inexpensive, easy to find, and will last for a long time.

X-Acto knife: The tiny blade on an X-Acto knife makes it perfect for cutting out shapes, getting into hard-to-reach places, and creating clean, precise cuts on fondant decorations.

Small rolling pin: A small rolling pin is ideal for rolling out small amounts of fondant.

Small paintbrush: A small paintbrush is used to attach candies and fondant, and it is perfect for applying gel colors and touching up mistakes.

Sprinkles and candies: The perfect adornment for themed cupcakes, sprinkles and candies add color and texture without altering the taste of the cupcake.

Fondant: A soft pliable sugar icing, fondant has the texture of playdough and the limitation of your imagination. It needs to be used at room temperature and must be kneaded before use. It can be colored, flavored, rolled, thinned, cut, pulled, molded, and dried to create any type of design. It has a light marshmallow taste and can be purchased or made. See page 132 for an easy-to-make marshmallow fondant that only takes minutes.

The Classics

Vanilla Bean Cupcakes

Nothings tastes better than a good simple cupcake. This vanilla bean cake is made with pure vanilla and vanilla bean paste. It is not overly sweet and has a light, tender crumb. It is the base recipe for many of our cupcakes, and simply put, it is a classic.

wet ingredients

¼ cup unsalted butter, softened
½ cup sour cream
¼ cup buttermilk
¼ cup unsweetened applesauce
½ cup vegetable oil
3 large eggs
2 Tbsp. pure vanilla
1 Tbsp. vanilla bean paste

dry ingredients

1 cup granulated sugar
2 cups all-purpose flour
1¼ Tbsp. baking powder
½ tsp. salt

Preparation

1. *Preheat oven* to 350 degrees.

2. *Beat butter* and sugar in the bowl of a stand mixer with the paddle attachment on medium speed until smooth. Stop mixer and scrape down the sides of the bowl. Add sour cream, buttermilk, applesauce, oil, eggs, vanilla, and vanilla bean paste. Mix until ingredients are well blended and smooth.

3. *In a* separate bowl, sift flour, baking powder, and salt.

4. *Turn the* stand mixer on low and add dry ingredients until just incorporated. The batter should be smooth

5. *Line two* standard muffin tins with paper cupcake liners. Fill each cup two-thirds full with batter. Use an ice cream scoop for perfect measuring. Bake until the tops spring back at the touch of your finger and the edges are just golden brown, 20–25 minutes.

6. *Remove from* tins and cool completely before filling or icing.

Finishing Touches: Ice with Vanilla Buttercream (118).

Unbeatable Chocolate Cupcakes

Made with melted dark chocolate and cocoa powder, this cake is rich, moist, and not too sweet, making it the ideal match for dark chocolate ganache, smooth chocolate buttercreams, and layers of fillings and garnishes.

wet ingredients

- ½ cup dark chocolate chopped into small pieces
- ½ cup boiling water
- ½ cup sour cream
- ½ cup unsweetened applesauce
- ½ cup vegetable oil
- 3 large eggs
- 1 Tbsp. pure vanilla

dry ingredients

- 1½ cups all-purpose flour
- 1 cup granulated sugar
- 1 Tbsp. baking powder
- ½ tsp. salt
- ½ cup Dutch-processed cocoa powder

Preparation

1. *Preheat oven* to 350 degrees.
2. *Place dark* chocolate in the bowl of a stand mixer. Pour boiling water over chocolate and let sit for 1 minute. Using the whisk attachment, mix until smooth. Scrape down the sides of the bowl.
3. *Add sour* cream, applesauce, oil, eggs, and vanilla.
3. *In a* separate bowl, sift flour, sugar, baking powder, salt, and cocoa.
4. *Turn the* stand mixer on low and add dry ingredients and mix until just incorporated. Batter should be smooth.
5. *Line two* standard muffin tins with paper cupcake liners. Fill each cup two-thirds full with batter. Use an ice cream scoop for perfect measuring. Bake until the tops spring back at the touch of your finger, and a toothpick inserted into the center comes out clean.
6. *Remove from* tins and cool completely before filling and icing.

Finishing Touches: Apply a single layer of Dark Chocolate Ganache (126), ice with Chocolate Buttercream (118), and garnish with a chocolate disc or chocolate curls.

NOTE: Be careful not to overfill your cupcake liners! These cupcakes will crown nicely, but if overfilled, the batter will spill over and create a "pocket" on the side of your cupcake.

Janell Brown

Sweet & Light

Coconut Key Lime Cupcakes

This recipe is the base for our famous Coconut Key Lime Cupcake. The coconut is mild and balances the tangy lime instead of overpowering it. This cupcake has a crisp buttery top and a moist tart center. It is perfect for cupcake lovers in the mood for something different.

wet ingredients

½ cup unsalted butter, softened
½ cup fresh lime juice
zest of 4 key limes
¼ cup milk
3 large eggs
2 Tbsp. pure vanilla
1 Tbsp. coconut extract

dry ingredients

1½ cups granulated sugar
2½ cups all-purpose flour
½ tsp. salt
2 Tbsp. baking powder

Preparation

1. *Preheat oven* to 350 degrees.

2. *Beat butter* and sugar in the bowl of a stand mixer with the paddle attachment on medium speed until smooth. Stop mixer and scrape down the sides of the bowl. Add lime juice, zest, milk, eggs, vanilla, and coconut extract. Mix until ingredients are well blended and smooth.

3. *In a* separate bowl, sift dry ingredients. Turn the stand mixer on low and add dry ingredients and mix until just incorporated. Batter should be smooth.

4. *Line two* standard muffin tins with paper cupcake liners. Fill each cup two-thirds full with batter. Use an ice cream scoop for perfect measuring. Bake until the tops spring back at the touch of your finger and the edges are just starting to brown, 20–25 minutes.

5. *Remove from* tins and cool completely before filling and icing.

Finishing Touches: Core center of cupcakes and fill with Lime Curd (127). Ice and garnish with sweetened coconut, lime wedge, or lime zest.

NOTE: If the baking powder is not sifted with the dry ingredients, it will begin to react with the citric acid and the batter will begin to bubble and quickly rise.

Sweet & Light

Raspberry Swirl Cupcakes

This cupcake is by far the summer wedding favorite! It combines a delicate vanilla cake and a fresh raspberry puree swirled together to create a marbled moist cupcake. No one can eat just one.

wet ingredients

¼ cup unsalted butter, softened
½ cup sour cream
¼ cup buttermilk
¼ cup unsweetened applesauce
½ cup vegetable oil
3 large eggs
2 Tbsp. pure vanilla
1 Tbsp. vanilla bean paste
½ cup raspberry puree (128)

dry ingredients

1 cup granulated sugar
¼ cup vanilla instant dry pudding mix
2 cups all-purpose flour
1¼ Tbsp. baking powder
½ tsp. salt

Preparation

1. *Preheat oven* to 350 degrees.

2. *Beat butter* and sugar in the bowl of a stand mixer with the paddle attachment on medium speed until smooth. Stop mixer and scrape down the sides of the bowl. Add sour cream, buttermilk, applesauce, oil, eggs, vanilla, and vanilla bean paste. Mix until ingredients are well blended and smooth.

3. *In a* separate bowl, sift dry vanilla pudding, flour, baking powder, and salt.

4. *Turn the* stand mixer on low and add dry ingredients until just incorporated. The batter should be smooth. Fold in raspberry puree until batter is marbled.

5. *Line two* standard muffin tins with paper cupcake liners. Fill each cup two-thirds full with batter. Use an ice cream scoop for perfect measuring. Bake until the tops spring back at the touch of your finger and the edges are just golden brown, 20–25 minutes.

6. *Remove from* tins and cool completely before filling or icing.

Finishing Touches: Ice with Cream Cheese Icing (120) and garnish with a single fresh raspberry.

NOTE: Be careful not to overmix when adding the raspberry puree. The batter should be marbled, not pink.

Janell Brown

Raspberry Lemonade Cupcakes

This cupcake shouts summer! Marbled layers of raspberry lemon cake, fresh lemon cream filling, and raspberry buttercream make this cupcake irresistible. Top it with crushed Lemonheads and a fresh raspberry to make it look as good as it tastes!

wet ingredients

½ cup unsalted butter, softened
½ cup fresh lemon juice
zest of 3 lemons
¼ cup milk
3 large eggs
2 Tbsp. pure vanilla
½ cup raspberry puree (128)

dry ingredients

1½ cups granulated sugar
2½ cups all-purpose flour
½ tsp. salt
2 Tbsp. baking powder

Preparation

1. *Preheat oven* to 350 degrees.

2. *Beat butter* and sugar in the bowl of a stand mixer with the paddle attachment on medium speed until smooth. Stop mixer and scrape down the sides of the bowl. Add lemon juice, zest, milk, eggs, and vanilla. Mix until ingredients are well blended and smooth.

3. *In a* separate bowl, sift dry ingredients. Turn the stand mixer on low and add dry ingredients and mix until just incorporated. Batter should be smooth.

4. *Fold in* raspberry puree. Do not overmix; batter should be marbled.

5. *Line four* standard muffin tins with paper cupcake liners. Fill each cup two-thirds full with batter. Use an ice cream scoop for perfect measuring. Bake until the tops spring back at the touch of your finger and the edges are just starting to brown, 20–25 minutes.

6. *Remove from* tins and cool completely before filling and icing.

Finishing Touches: Core center of cupcake and fill with Lemon Cream (127), ice with Raspberry Buttercream (119), and garnish with crushed Lemonheads and a single fresh raspberry.

NOTE: This cupcake is dense. It will not rise as high as other cupcakes due to the added moisture of the raspberry puree. Be sure to fill your liners just past the ²/₃ mark to have a fully rounded top on your cupcake.

Sweet & Light

Raspberry Almond Poppy Seed Cupcakes

This cupcake is a twist on a summertime favorite. Fresh raspberries, swirled into almond poppy seed batter, and topped with a raspberry buttercream, crushed almonds, and a fresh raspberry. Delicious!

wet ingredients

¼ cup unsalted butter, softened
½ cup sour cream
¼ cup buttermilk
¼ cup unsweetened applesauce
½ cup vegetable oil
3 large eggs
2 Tbsp. pure vanilla
1 Tbsp. vanilla bean paste
1 Tbsp. almond extract
½ cup raspberry puree (128)

dry ingredients

1 cup granulated sugar
2 cups all-purpose flour
1¼ Tbsp. baking powder
½ tsp. salt
2 Tbsp. poppy seeds

Preparation

1. *Preheat the* oven to 350 degrees.

2. *Beat butter* and sugar in the bowl of a stand mixer with the paddle attachment on medium speed until smooth. Stop mixer and scrape down the sides of the bowl. Add sour cream, buttermilk, applesauce, oil, eggs, vanilla, vanilla bean paste, and almond extract. Mix until ingredients are well blended and smooth.

3. *In a* separate bowl, sift flour, baking powder, salt, and poppy seeds.

4. *Turn the* stand mixer on low and add dry ingredients until just incorporated. The batter should be smooth. Fold in raspberry puree until batter is marbled.

5. *Line two* standard muffin tins with paper cupcake liners. Fill each cup two-thirds full with batter. Use an ice cream scoop for perfect measuring. Bake until the tops spring back at the touch of your finger and the edges are just golden brown, 20–25 minutes.

6. *Remove from* tins and cool completely before filling or icing.

Finishing Touches: Ice with Raspberry Buttercream (119) and garnish with crushed almonds and a single fresh raspberry.

NOTE: Be careful not to overmix when adding the raspberry puree. The batter should be marbled, not pink.

Janell Brown

Lavender Honey Cupcakes

This is the perfect cupcake to serve at a brunch, afternoon party, or outdoor wedding. It is simple but elegant, unique but tasteful, and a flavor that everyone will talk about and love.

wet ingredients

¼ cup unsalted butter, softened
½ cup sour cream
¼ cup buttermilk
¼ cup unsweetened applesauce
½ cup vegetable oil
3 large eggs
3 drops lavender oil
2 Tbsp. pure vanilla
1 Tbsp. vanilla bean paste

dry ingredients

1 cup granulated sugar
2 cups all-purpose flour
1¼ Tbsp. baking powder
½ tsp. salt
2 Tbsp. dried lavender

Preparation

1. *Preheat the* oven to 350 degrees.

2. *Beat butter* and sugar in the bowl of a stand mixer with the paddle attachment on medium speed until smooth. Stop mixer and scrape down the sides of the bowl. Add sour cream, buttermilk, applesauce, oil, eggs, lavender oil, vanilla, and vanilla bean paste. Mix until ingredients are well blended and smooth.

3. *In a* separate bowl, sift flour, baking powder, and salt.

4. *Turn the* stand mixer on low and add dry ingredients mixture until just incorporated. The batter should be smooth. Fold in dried lavender.

5. *Line two* standard muffin tins with paper cupcake liners. Fill each cup two-thirds full with batter. Use an ice cream scoop for perfect measuring. Bake until the tops spring back at the touch of your finger and the edges are just golden brown, 20–25 minutes.

6. *Remove from* tins and cool completely before filling or icing.

Finishing Touches: Ice with Honey Cream Cheese (121) and garnish with fresh or dried lavender.

NOTE: Be careful to add only a small amount of the lavender oil. It is very powerful and is used in healing. Too much lavender will make your cupcake taste like floral soap.

Pink Grapefruit Cupcakes

This cupcake is so light and refreshing it almost shouldn't be called cake! The grapefruit cream cheese is the perfect twist to make this cupcake a balance between tart and tangy. This cupcake is light, feminine, and irresistible.

wet ingredients

½ cup unsalted butter, softened
½ cup fresh grapefruit juice
2 Tbsp. pink grapefruit zest
¼ cup milk
3 large eggs
2 Tbsp. pure vanilla

dry ingredients

1½ cups granulated sugar
2½ cups all-purpose flour
½ tsp. salt
2 Tbsp. baking powder

Preparation

1. *Preheat oven* to 350 degrees.

2. *Beat butter* and sugar in the bowl of a stand mixer with the paddle attachment on medium speed until smooth. Stop mixer and scrape down the sides of the bowl. Add grapefruit juice, zest, milk, eggs, and vanilla. Mix until ingredients are well blended and smooth.

3. *Sift dry* ingredients in a separate bowl. Turn the stand mixer on low and add dry ingredients and mix until just incorporated. Batter should be smooth.

4. *Line two* standard muffin tins with paper cupcake liners. Fill each cup two-thirds full with batter. Use an ice cream scoop for perfect measuring. Bake until the tops spring back at the touch of your finger and the edges are just starting to brown, 20–25 minutes.

5. *Remove from* tins and cool completely before filling and icing.

Finishing Touches: Ice cupcakes with Grapefruit Cream Cheese (121), and garnish with grapefruit zest.

NOTE: Add a drop of pink food coloring to the icing to give this cupcake a feminine touch without affecting the flavor.

Janell Brown

Coconut Mango Cupcakes

Adding mango to a coconut cupcake is a great way to bring in the summer whatever the time of year may be! This cupcake has a refreshing tropical taste and reminds me of the warm sun every time I bite into one.

wet ingredients

- ¼ cup unsalted butter, softened
- ½ cup sour cream
- ¼ cup buttermilk
- ¼ cup unsweetened applesauce
- ½ cup vegetable oil
- 3 large eggs
- 2 Tbsp. pure vanilla
- 2 Tbsp. coconut extract
- ⅓ cup mango puree (128)
- 1 cup shredded coconut

dry ingredients

- 1 cup granulated sugar
- 2 cups all-purpose flour
- 1¼ Tbsp. baking powder
- ½ tsp. salt

Preparation

1. *Preheat oven* to 350 degrees.
2. *Beat butter* and sugar in the bowl of a stand mixer with the paddle attachment on medium speed until smooth. Stop mixer and scrape down the sides of the bowl. Add sour cream, buttermilk, applesauce, oil, eggs, vanilla, and coconut extract. Mix until ingredients are well blended and smooth.
3. *In a* separate bowl, sift flour, baking powder, and salt.
4. *Turn the* stand mixer on low and add dry ingredients until just incorporated. The batter should be smooth.
5. *Mix in* mango puree until fully blended. Fold in shredded coconut.
6. *Line two* standard muffin tins with paper cupcake liners. Fill each cup two-thirds full with batter. Use an ice cream scoop for perfect measuring. Bake until the tops spring back at the touch of your finger and the edges are just golden brown, 20–25 minutes.
7. *Remove from* tins and cool completely before filling or icing.

Finishing Touches: Ice with Coconut Cream Cheese (121) and garnish with shredded coconut.

Sweet & Light

Banana Cupcakes

These cupcakes can be topped and served multiple ways. My favorite is layered with peanut butter cream and chocolate buttercream. Any way you top it, this banana cupcake is quickly devoured every time!

wet ingredients

- ½ cup unsalted butter, softened
- ½ cup sour cream
- ¼ cup buttermilk
- ¼ cup unsweetened applesauce
- ½ cup vegetable oil
- 4 large eggs
- 1 Tbsp. pure vanilla
- 4 ripe bananas, peeled and mashed

dry ingredients

- 1½ cups granulated sugar
- 2½ cups all-purpose flour
- 1¼ cups brown sugar
- 1¼ Tbsp. baking powder
- ½ tsp. salt
- 1 tsp. ground cinnamon

Preparation

1. *Preheat oven* to 350 degrees.

2. *Beat butter* and sugar in the bowl of a stand mixer with the paddle attachment on medium speed until smooth. Stop mixer and scrape down the sides of the bowl.

Add sour cream, buttermilk, applesauce, oil, eggs, vanilla, and mashed bananas. Mix until ingredients are well blended and smooth.

3. *In a* separate bowl, sift flour, brown sugar, baking powder, salt, and cinnamon.

4. *Turn the* stand mixer on low and add dry ingredients until just incorporated. The batter should be smooth.

5. *Line two* standard muffin tins with paper cupcake liners. Fill each cup two-thirds full with batter. Use an ice cream scoop for perfect measuring. Bake until the tops spring back at the touch of your finger and the edges are just golden brown, 20–25 minutes.

6. *Remove from* tins and cool completely before filling or icing.

Finishing Touches: Ice with a small layer of Peanut Butter Cream (118) and top with Chocolate Buttercream (118) and a banana chip.

Janell Brown

32

Lemon Blueberry Cupcakes

This is the cupcake I reach for whenever I want to feel like I'm making a healthier choice! It's loaded with fresh blueberries and real lemons, and it's packed with a tangy lemon cream.

wet ingredients

½ cup unsalted butter, softened
½ cup fresh lemon juice
zest of 3 lemons
¼ cup milk
3 large eggs
2 Tbsp. pure vanilla
½ cup fresh blueberries

dry ingredients

1½ cups granulated sugar
2½ cups all-purpose flour
½ tsp. salt
2 Tbsp. baking powder

Preparation

1. *Preheat oven* to 350 degrees.

2. *Beat butter* and sugar in the bowl of a stand mixer with the paddle attachment on medium speed until smooth. Stop mixer and scrape down the sides of the bowl. Add lemon juice, zest, milk, eggs, and vanilla. Mix until ingredients are well blended and smooth.

3. *Sift dry* ingredients in a separate bowl. Turn the stand mixer on low and add dry ingredients and mix until just incorporated. Batter should be smooth.

4. *Fold in* blueberries.

5. *Line two* standard muffin tins with paper cupcake liners. Fill each cup two-thirds full with batter. Use an ice cream scoop for perfect measuring. Bake until the tops spring back at the touch of your finger and the edges are just starting to brown, 20-25 minutes.

6. *Remove from* tins and cool completely before filling and icing.

Finishing Touches: Core center of cupcakes and fill with Lemon Cream (127). Ice with Lemon Cream Cheese (121) and top with a fresh blueberry.

NOTE: To keep your blueberries from sinking to the bottom of the cupcake liners, fill a bag with a small amount of flour, pour your blueberries in, and shake! Coating the berries in flour helps keep them anchored in the batter so they don't fall to the bottom while the cupcakes bake.

Strawberry Margarita Cupcakes

These cupcakes are the center of any good party! Tart lime cupcakes marbled with strawberry puree, filled with a fresh lime curd, and topped with a strawberry buttercream and salt—you wont be able to have just one.

wet ingredients

½ cup unsalted butter, softened
½ cup fresh lime juice
zest of 3 limes
¼ cup milk
3 large eggs
2 Tbsp. pure vanilla
½ cup strawberry puree (128)

dry ingredients

1½ cups granulated sugar
2½ cups all-purpose flour
½ tsp. salt
2 Tbsp. baking powder

Preparation

1. *Preheat oven* to 350 degrees.

2. *Beat butter* and sugar in the bowl of a stand mixer with the paddle attachment on medium speed until smooth. Stop mixer and scrape down the sides of the bowl. Add lime juice, zest, milk, eggs, and vanilla. Mix until ingredients are well blended and smooth.

3. *Sift dry* ingredients in a separate bowl. Turn the stand mixer on low and add dry ingredients and mix until just incorporated. Batter should be smooth.

4. *Fold in* strawberry puree and stir until marbled.

5. *Line two* standard muffin tins with paper cupcake liners. Fill each cup two-thirds full with batter. Use an ice cream scoop for perfect measuring. Bake until the tops spring back at the touch of your finger and the edges are just starting to brown, 20–25 minutes.

6. *Remove from* tins and cool completely before filling and icing.

Finishing Touches: Core center of cupcakes and fill with Lime Curd (127), ice with Strawberry Buttercream (119), and garnish with lime wedges, strawberry halves, and kosher salt.

Janell Brown

Orange Blossom Cupcakes

This is a light almond orange cake with fresh orange zest throughout the batter. The texture is moist and tender and reminds me of the first blossoms of spring.

wet ingredients

- ¼ cup unsalted butter, softened
- 2 Tbsp. orange zest
- ½ cup sour cream
- ¼ cup buttermilk
- ¼ cup orange juice
- ¼ cup unsweetened applesauce
- ½ cup vegetable oil
- 3 large eggs
- 2 Tbsp. pure vanilla
- 1 Tbsp. almond extract

dry ingredients

- 1 cup granulated sugar
- 2 cups all-purpose flour
- 1¼ Tbsp. baking powder
- ½ tsp. salt

Preparation

1. *Preheat oven* to 350 degrees.

2. *Beat butter* and sugar in the bowl of a stand mixer with the paddle attachment on medium speed until smooth. Stop mixer and scrape down the sides of the bowl. Add orange zest, sour cream, buttermilk, orange juice, applesauce, oil, eggs, vanilla, and almond extract. Mix until ingredients are well blended and smooth.

3. *In a* separate bowl, sift flour, baking powder, and salt.

4. *Turn the* stand mixer on low and add dry ingredients until just incorporated. The batter should be smooth.

5. *Line two* standard muffin tins with paper cupcake liners. Fill each cup two-thirds full with batter. Use an ice cream scoop for perfect measuring. Bake until the tops spring back at the touch of your finger and the edges are just golden brown, 20–25 minutes.

6. *Remove from* tins and cool completely before filling or icing.

Finishing Touches: Ice with Orange Cream Cheese (121) and garnish with a sugar flower.

Sweet & Light

39

Lemon Poppy Seed Cupcakes

This cupcake is not too sweet and is perfect for those cupcake lovers who like less icing. The bold flavor of the lemon cake flecked with black poppy seeds creates a beautiful contrast that tastes as good as it looks!

wet ingredients

½ cup unsalted butter, softened
½ cup fresh lemon juice
zest of 3 lemons
¼ cup milk
3 large eggs
2 Tbsp. pure vanilla

dry ingredients

1½ cups granulated sugar
2½ cups all-purpose flour
½ tsp. salt
2 Tbsp. baking powder
2 Tbsp. poppy seeds

Preparation

1. *Preheat oven* to 350 degrees.

2. *Beat butter* and sugar in the bowl of a stand mixer with the paddle attachment on medium speed until smooth. Stop mixer and scrape down the sides of the bowl. Add lemon juice, zest, milk, eggs, and vanilla. Mix until ingredients are well blended and smooth.

3. *Sift dry* ingredients in a separate bowl. Turn the stand mixer on low and add dry ingredients and mix until just incorporated. Batter should be smooth.

4. *Line four* standard muffin tins with paper cupcake liners. Fill each cup two-thirds full with batter. Use an ice cream scoop for perfect measuring. Bake until the tops spring back at the touch of your finger and the edges are just starting to brown, 20–25 minutes.

5. *Remove from* tins and cool completely before filling and icing.

Finishing Touches: Ice with Citrus Glaze (117) and garnish with lemon zest.

Janell Brown

Blackberry Cupcakes

The flavors of this cupcake hint at the summer mountainside. Fresh blackberries blended into vanilla bean batter and then repeated in the icing creates a delicious experience.

wet ingredients

- ¼ cup unsalted butter, softened
- ½ cup sour cream
- ¼ cup buttermilk
- ¼ cup unsweetened applesauce
- ½ cup vegetable oil
- 3 large eggs
- 2 Tbsp. pure vanilla
- 1 Tbsp. vanilla bean paste
- ½ cup blackberry puree (128)

dry ingredients

- 1 cup granulated sugar
- 2 cups all-purpose flour
- 1¼ Tbsp. baking powder
- ½ tsp. salt

Preparation

1. Preheat oven to 350 degrees.
2. Beat butter and sugar in the bowl of a stand mixer with the paddle attachment on medium speed until smooth. Stop mixer and scrape down the sides of the bowl. Add sour cream, buttermilk, applesauce, oil, eggs, vanilla, and vanilla bean paste. Mix until ingredients are well blended and smooth.
3. In a separate bowl, sift flour, baking powder, and salt.
4. Turn the stand mixer on low and add dry ingredients until just incorporated. The batter should be smooth. Fold in blackberry puree until batter is marbled.
5. Line two standard muffin tins with paper cupcake liners. Fill each cup two-thirds full with batter. Use an ice cream scoop for perfect measuring. Bake until the tops spring back at the touch of your finger and the edges are just golden brown, 20–25 minutes.
6. Remove from tins and cool completely before filling or icing.

Finishing Touches: Ice with Blackberry Buttercream (119) and garnish with a single fresh blackberry.

NOTE: Be careful not to overmix when adding the blackberry puree. The batter should be marbled.

Piña Colada Cupcakes

Pineapple and coconut meet together in this tropical paradise of a cupcake. The cake is thick, moist, and textured with shredded coconut. The coconut milk in the icing creates a light and creamy complement to this summertime favorite.

wet ingredients

- ¼ cup unsalted butter, softened
- ½ cup sour cream
- ¼ cup buttermilk
- ¼ cup pineapple juice
- ¼ cup unsweetened applesauce
- ½ cup vegetable oil
- 3 large eggs
- 2 Tbsp. pure vanilla
- 2 Tbsp. coconut extract
- 1 cup shredded coconut
- 1 (8-oz.) can crushed pineapple, drained

dry ingredients

- 1 cup granulated sugar
- 2 cups all-purpose flour
- 1¼ Tbsp. baking powder
- ½ tsp. salt

Preparation

1. *Preheat oven* to 350 degrees.

2. *Beat butter* and sugar in the bowl of a stand mixer with the paddle attachment on medium speed until smooth. Stop mixer and scrape down the sides of the bowl. Add sour cream, buttermilk, pineapple juice, applesauce, oil, eggs, vanilla, and coconut extract. Mix until ingredients are well blended and smooth.

3. *In a* separate bowl, sift flour, baking powder, and salt.

4. *Turn the* stand mixer on low and add dry ingredients until just incorporated. The batter should be smooth.

5. *Fold in* shredded coconut and crushed pineapple.

6. *Line two* standard muffin tins with paper cupcake liners. Fill each cup two-thirds full with batter. Use an ice cream scoop for perfect measuring. Bake until the tops spring back at the touch of your finger and the edges are just golden brown, 20–25 minutes.

7. *Remove from* tins and cool completely before filling or icing.

Finishing Touches: Ice with Coconut Cream Cheese (121) and garnish with shredded coconut and a maraschino cherry.

Janell Brown

Strawberries and Cream Cupcakes

MAKES 24 Standard-Size Cupcakes

This cupcake is perfect for a garden party, picnic, or afternoon with the girls. It is moist and not overly sweet, with a perfect mound of whipped cream and a fresh strawberry slice on top.

wet ingredients

- ¼ cup unsalted butter, softened
- ½ cup sour cream
- ¼ cup buttermilk
- ¼ cup unsweetened applesauce
- ½ cup vegetable oil
- 3 large eggs
- 2 Tbsp. pure vanilla
- 1 Tbsp. vanilla bean paste
- ½ cup strawberry puree (128)

dry ingredients

- 1 cup granulated sugar
- 2 cups all-purpose flour
- 1¼ Tbsp. baking powder
- ½ tsp. salt

Preparation

1. *Preheat oven* to 350 degrees.

2. *Beat butter* and sugar in the bowl of a stand mixer with the paddle attachment on medium speed until smooth. Stop mixer and scrape down the sides of the bowl.

Add sour cream, buttermilk, applesauce, oil, eggs, vanilla, and vanilla bean paste. Mix until ingredients are well blended and smooth.

3. *In a* separate bowl sift flour, baking powder, and salt.

4. *Turn the* stand mixer on low and add dry ingredients until just incorporated. The batter should be smooth. Fold in strawberry puree until batter is marbled.

5. *Line two* standard muffin tins with paper cupcake liners. Fill each cup two-thirds full with batter. Use an ice cream scoop for perfect measuring. Bake until the tops spring back at the touch of your finger and the edges are just golden brown, 20–25 minutes.

6. *Remove from* tins and cool completely before filling or icing.

Finishing Touches: Ice with Fresh Whipped Cream (117) and then garnish with a sliced strawberry.

NOTE: Be careful not to overmix when adding the strawberry puree. The batter should be marbled, not pink.

Sweet & Light

47

Peaches and Cream Cupcakes

A thick, juicy peach, fresh whipped cream, and a touch of nutmeg make this cupcake perfect for late summer lunches or evening desserts. The secret to this cupcake is in the fresh peach and the lightly spiced cake, baked in summer but giving hints of fall flavors to come.

wet ingredients

¼ cup unsalted butter, softened
½ cup sour cream
¼ cup buttermilk
¼ cup unsweetened applesauce
½ cup vegetable oil
3 large eggs
2 Tbsp. pure vanilla
1 Tbsp. vanilla bean paste

dry ingredients

1 cup granulated sugar
2 cups all-purpose flour
2 Tbsp. brown sugar
¼ tsp. nutmeg
¼ tsp. cinnamon
1¼ Tbsp. baking powder
½ tsp. salt

Preparation

1. *Preheat oven* to 350 degrees.

2. *Beat butter* and sugar in the bowl of a stand mixer with the paddle attachment on medium speed until smooth. Stop mixer and scrape down the sides of the bowl. Add sour cream, buttermilk, applesauce, oil, eggs, vanilla, and vanilla bean paste. Mix until ingredients are well blended and smooth.

3. *In a* separate bowl sift flour, brown sugar, spices, baking powder, and salt.

4. *Turn the* stand mixer on low and add dry ingredients until just incorporated. The batter should be smooth.

5. *Line 2* standard muffin tins with paper cupcake liners. Fill each cup two-thirds full with batter. Use an ice cream scoop for perfect measuring. Bake until the tops spring back at the touch of your finger and the edges are just golden brown, 20–25 minutes.

6. *Remove from* tins and cool completely before filling or icing.

Finishing Touches: Ice with Fresh Whipped Cream (117), nutmeg, and a peach slice.

Janell Brown

Cranberry Orange Cupcakes

This cupcake is the perfect introduction to fall. The light citrus flavor of the orange leaves a taste of summer while the fresh cranberries get your taste buds ready for the rich flavors of fall!

wet ingredients

- ¼ cup unsalted butter, softened
- 2 Tbsp. orange zest
- ½ cup sour cream
- ¼ cup buttermilk
- ¼ cup orange juice
- ¼ cup unsweetened applesauce
- ½ cup vegetable oil
- 3 large eggs
- 2 Tbsp. pure vanilla
- ¾ cup fresh whole cranberries (not canned)

dry ingredients

- 1 cup granulated sugar
- 2 cups all-purpose flour
- 1¼ Tbsp. baking powder
- ½ tsp. salt

Preparation

1. *Preheat oven* to 350 degrees.

2. *Beat butter* and sugar in the bowl of a stand mixer with the paddle attachment on medium speed until smooth. Stop mixer and scrape down the sides of the bowl. Add orange zest, sour cream, buttermilk, orange juice, applesauce, oil, eggs, and vanilla. Mix until ingredients are well blended and smooth.

3. *In a* separate bowl sift flour, baking powder, and salt.

4. *Turn the* stand mixer on low and add dry ingredients until just incorporated. The batter should be smooth. Fold in whole cranberries.

5. *Line two* standard muffin tins with paper cupcake liners. Fill each cup two-thirds full with batter. Use an ice cream scoop for perfect measuring. Bake until the tops spring back at the touch of your finger and the edges are just golden brown, 20–25 minutes.

6. *Remove from* tins and cool completely before filling or icing.

Finishing Touches: Ice with Citrus Glaze (117), orange zest, and dried cranberries.

NOTE: To keep cranberries from sinking to the bottom of the liners, fill a bag with a small amount of flour, pour your cranberries in, and shake! Coating the berries in flour keeps them anchored in the batter so they don't fall to the bottom during baking.

Sweet & Light

51

Ginger Pear Cupcakes

Whenever I hear the name of this cupcake, I picture warm ginger molasses cupcakes with slices of sweet pears and a light sugar glaze. This cupcake is warm and invites you at every bite to eat more than just one.

wet ingredients

¼ cup unsalted butter, softened
½ cup sour cream
¼ cup buttermilk
¼ cup unsweetened applesauce
½ cup vegetable oil
3 large eggs
2 Tbsp. pure vanilla
½ cup molasses
1 large ripe pear, peeled and
  chopped

dry ingredients

1 cup granulated sugar
¼ cup brown sugar
2 cups all-purpose flour
2 tsp. dry ginger
2 tsp. cinnamon
½ tsp. ground cloves
¼ tsp. nutmeg
1¼ Tbsp. baking powder
½ tsp. salt

Preparation

1. *Preheat oven* to 350 degrees.

2. *Beat butter* and sugar in the bowl of a stand mixer with the paddle attachment on medium speed until smooth. Stop mixer and scrape down the sides of the bowl. Add sour cream, buttermilk, applesauce, oil, eggs, vanilla, molasses, and brown sugar. Mix until ingredients are well blended and smooth.

3. *In a* separate bowl sift flour, spices, baking powder, and salt.

4. *Turn the* stand mixer on low and add dry ingredients until just incorporated. The batter should be smooth.

5. *Fold in* peeled and chopped pears (about 1 cup).

6. *Line two* standard muffin tins with paper cupcake liners. Fill each cup two-thirds full with batter. Use an ice cream scoop for perfect measuring. Bake until the tops spring back at the touch of your finger and the edges are just golden brown, 20–25 minutes.

7. *Remove from* tins and cool completely before filling or icing.

Finishing Touches: Ice with Molasses Cream Cheese (122) and top with ginger and a pear slice.

White Chocolate Raspberry Cupcakes

I always think of Valentine's Day when I taste these cupcakes. Lighter than the Chocolate Raspberry (66), it has a decadent flavor without being overbearing. The raspberry swirled cake layered with white chocolate ganache and white chocolate buttercream and garnished with a fresh raspberry will make these a hit every time.

wet ingredients

- ¼ cup unsalted butter, softened
- ½ cup sour cream
- ¼ cup buttermilk
- ¼ cup unsweetened applesauce
- ½ cup vegetable oil
- 3 large eggs
- 2 Tbsp. pure vanilla
- 1 Tbsp. vanilla bean paste
- ½ cup raspberry puree (128)

dry ingredients

- 1 cup granulated sugar
- 2 cups all-purpose flour
- 1¼ Tbsp. baking powder
- ½ tsp. salt

Preparation

1. *Preheat oven* to 350 degrees.
2. *Beat butter* and sugar in the bowl of a stand mixer with the paddle attachment on medium speed until smooth. Stop mixer and scrape down the sides of the bowl. Add sour cream, buttermilk, applesauce, oil, eggs, vanilla, and vanilla bean paste. Mix until ingredients are well blended and smooth.
3. *In a* separate bowl, sift flour, baking powder, and salt.
4. *Turn the* stand mixer on low and add dry ingredients until just incorporated. The batter should be smooth. Fold in raspberry puree until batter is marbled.
5. *Line two* standard muffin tins with paper cupcake liners. Fill each cup two-thirds full with batter. Use an ice cream scoop for perfect measuring. Bake until the tops spring back at the touch of your finger and the edges are just golden brown, 20–25 minutes.
6. *Remove from* tins and cool completely before filling or icing.

Finishing Touches: Pipe a layer of White Chocolate Ganache (126), ice with White Chocolate Buttercream (118), and roll in white chocolate flakes. Garnish with a single fresh raspberry.

NOTE: Be careful not to overmix when adding the raspberry puree. The batter should be marbled, not pink.

Sweet & Light

55

The Dark Side

Orange Chocolate Cupcakes

This rich, tangy cupcake combines the flavor of citrus and dark chocolate to create a winter favorite. Topped with orange cream cheese and chocolate curls, this cupcake looks as good as it tastes.

wet ingredients

- ½ cup dark chocolate chopped into small pieces
- ½ cup boiling water
- ½ cup sour cream
- ½ cup unsweetened applesauce
- ½ cup vegetable oil
- 3 large eggs
- 1 Tbsp. pure vanilla
- 1 Tbsp. orange extract

dry ingredients

- 1½ cups all-purpose flour
- 1 cup granulated sugar
- 1 Tbsp. baking powder
- ½ tsp. salt
- ½ cup Dutch-processed cocoa powder

Preparation

1. *Preheat oven* to 350 degrees.

2. *Place chocolate* in the bowl of a stand mixer. Pour boiling water over chocolate and let sit for 1 minute. Using the whisk attachment, mix until smooth. Scrape down the sides of the bowl.

3. *Add sour* cream, applesauce, oil, eggs, vanilla, and orange extract.

4. *In a* separate bowl, sift flour, sugar, baking powder, salt, and cocoa powder.

5. *Turn the* stand mixer on low and add dry ingredients and mix until just incorporated. Batter should be smooth.

6. *Line two* standard muffin tins with paper cupcake liners. Fill each cup two-thirds full with batter. Use an ice cream scoop for perfect measuring. Bake until the tops spring back at the touch of your finger and a toothpick inserted into the center comes out clean.

7. *Remove from* tins and cool completely before icing.

Finishing Touches: Apply a single layer of Dark Chocolate Ganache (126), ice with Orange Cream Cheese (121), and garnish with chocolate curls.

Grasshopper Cupcakes

This cupcake is a favorite of children and adults alike. Filled with mint chocolate ganache and topped with a mint Oreo buttercream, the crumbs will be licked off the plate!

wet ingredients

- ½ cup dark chocolate chopped into small pieces
- ½ cup boiling water
- ½ cup sour cream
- ½ cup unsweetened applesauce
- ½ cup vegetable oil
- 3 large eggs
- 1 Tbsp. pure vanilla

dry ingredients

- 1½ cups all-purpose flour
- 1 cup granulated sugar
- 1 Tbsp. baking powder
- ½ tsp. salt
- ½ cup Dutch-processed cocoa powder

Preparation

1. *Preheat oven* to 350 degrees.

2. *Place chocolate* in the bowl of a stand mixer. Pour boiling water over chocolate and let sit for 1 minute. Using the whisk attachment, mix until smooth. Scrape down the sides of the bowl.

3. *Add sour* cream, applesauce, oil, eggs, and vanilla.

4. *In a* separate bowl, sift flour, sugar, baking powder, salt, and cocoa powder.

5. *Turn the* stand mixer on low and add dry ingredients and mix until just incorporated. Batter should be smooth.

6. *Line two* standard muffin tins with paper cupcake liners. Fill each cup two-thirds full with batter. Use an ice cream scoop for perfect measuring. Bake until the tops spring back at the touch of your finger and a toothpick inserted into the center comes out clean.

7. *Remove from* tins and cool completely before filling and icing.

Finishing Touches: Core center of cupcakes and fill with Mint Chocolate Ganache (126). Ice with Grasshopper Buttercream (119).

The Dark Side

Chocolate Fleur de Sel Cupcakes

Salt of the sea is the key flavor in this cupcake. Filled with caramel filling, iced with chocolate butter-cream, and drizzled in caramel and salt. The combination of sweet and salty makes the first bite as good as the last.

wet ingredients

½ cup dark chocolate chopped into
    small pieces
½ cup boiling water
½ cup sour cream
½ cup unsweetened applesauce
½ cup vegetable oil
3 large eggs
1 Tbsp. pure vanilla

dry ingredients

1½ cups all-purpose flour
1 cup granulated sugar
1 Tbsp. baking powder
½ tsp. salt
½ cup Dutch-processed cocoa
    powder

Preparation

1. *Preheat oven* to 350 degrees.

2. *Place chocolate* in the bowl of a stand mixer. Pour boiling water over chocolate and let sit for 1 minute. Using the whisk attachment, mix until smooth. Scrape down the sides of the bowl.

3. *Add sour* cream, applesauce, oil, eggs, and vanilla.

4. *In a* separate bowl, sift flour, sugar, baking powder, salt, and cocoa powder.

5. *Turn the* stand mixer on low and add dry ingredients and mix until just incorporated. Batter should be smooth.

6. *Line four* standard muffin tins with paper cupcake liners. Fill each cup two-thirds full with batter. Use an ice cream scoop for perfect measuring. Bake until the tops spring back at the touch of your finger and a toothpick inserted into the center comes out clean.

7. *Remove from* tins and cool completely before filling and icing.

Finishing Touches: Core the center of the cupcake and fill with Caramel Filling (126) and salt. Ice with Chocolate Buttercream (118), drizzle with caramel, and garnish with salt.

Janell Brown

62

Peanut Butter Swirl Cupcakes

This cupcake needs a cold glass of milk to help finish it off. Chocolate cake swirled with peanut butter, layered with a peanut butter cream, iced with a chocolate buttercream, and topped with a peanut butter cup.

wet ingredients

- ½ cup dark chocolate chopped into small pieces
- ½ cup boiling water
- ½ cup sour cream
- ½ cup unsweetened applesauce
- ½ cup vegetable oil
- 3 large eggs
- 1 Tbsp. pure vanilla
- Peanut Butter Filling (128)

dry ingredients

- 1½ cups all-purpose flour
- 1 cup granulated sugar
- 1 Tbsp. baking powder
- ½ tsp. salt
- ½ cup Dutch-processed cocoa powder

Preparation

1. *Preheat oven* to 350 degrees.

2. *Place chocolate* in the bowl of a stand mixer. Pour boiling water over chocolate and let sit for 1 minute. Using the whisk attachment, mix until smooth. Scrape down the sides of the bowl.

3. *Add sour* cream, applesauce, oil, eggs, and vanilla.

4. *In a* separate bowl sift flour, sugar, baking powder, salt, and cocoa powder.

5. *Turn the* stand mixer on low and add dry ingredients and mix until just incorporated. Batter should be smooth.

6. *Stir in* peanut butter filling and mix until marbled.

7. *Line two* standard muffin tins with paper cupcake liners. Fill each cup two-thirds full with batter. Use an ice cream scoop for perfect measuring. Bake until the tops spring back at the touch of your finger and a toothpick inserted into the center comes out clean.

8. *Remove from* tins and cool completely before filling and icing.

Finishing Touches: Apply a single layer of Peanut Butter Cream (118), ice with Chocolate Buttercream (118), and garnish with a peanut butter cup.

Chocolate Raspberry Cupcakes

This is my husband's all-time favorite cupcake. Moist chocolate cake swirled with a fresh raspberry puree, layered with dark chocolate ganache, iced with raspberry buttercream, and topped with a fresh raspberry. Delicious.

wet ingredients

½ cup dark chocolate chopped into small pieces
½ cup boiling water
½ cup sour cream
½ cup unsweetened applesauce
½ cup vegetable oil
3 large eggs
1 Tbsp. pure vanilla
½ cup raspberry puree (128)

dry ingredients

1½ cups all-purpose flour
1 cup granulated sugar
1 Tbsp. baking powder
½ tsp. salt
½ cup Dutch-processed cocoa powder

Preparation

1. *Preheat oven* to 350 degrees.

2. *Place chocolate* in the bowl of a stand mixer. Pour boiling water over chocolate and let sit for 1 minute. Using the whisk attachment, mix until smooth. Scrape down the sides of the bowl.

3. *Add sour* cream, applesauce, oil, eggs, and vanilla.

4. *In a* separate bowl, sift flour, sugar, baking powder, salt, and cocoa powder.

5. *Turn the* stand mixer on low and add dry ingredients and mix until just incorporated. Batter should be smooth.

6. *Fold in* raspberry puree until marbled.

7. *Line two* standard muffin tins with paper cupcake liners. Fill each cup two-thirds full with batter. Use an ice cream scoop for perfect measuring. Bake until the tops spring back at the touch of your finger and a toothpick inserted into the center comes out clean.

8. *Remove from* tins and cool completely before filling and icing.

Finishing Touches: Apply a single layer of Dark Chocolate Ganache (126), ice with Raspberry Buttercream (119), and garnish with a fresh raspberry.

Janell Brown

Samoa Cupcakes

Named after the Girl Scout cookies, these cupcakes are loaded with chocolate, coconut, and caramel. Just looking at them is enough to make your mouth water!

wet ingredients

- ½ cup dark chocolate chopped into small pieces
- ½ cup boiling water
- ½ cup sour cream
- ½ cup unsweetened applesauce
- ½ cup vegetable oil
- 3 large eggs
- 1 Tbsp. pure vanilla
- ½ cup shredded coconut

dry ingredients

- 1½ cups all-purpose flour
- 1 cup granulated sugar
- 1 Tbsp. baking powder
- ½ tsp. salt
- ½ cup Dutch-processed cocoa powder

Preparation

1. *Preheat oven* to 350 degrees.
2. *Place chocolate* in the bowl of a stand mixer. Pour boiling water over chocolate and let sit for 1 minute. Using the whisk attachment, mix until smooth. Scrape down the sides of the bowl.
3. *Add sour* cream, applesauce, oil, eggs, and vanilla.
4. *In a* separate bowl, sift flour, sugar, baking powder, salt, and cocoa powder.
5. *Fold in* shredded coconut.
6. *Turn the* stand mixer on low and add dry ingredients and mix until just incorporated. Batter should be smooth.
7. *Line two* standard muffin tins with paper cupcake liners. Fill each cup two-thirds full with batter. Use an ice cream scoop for perfect measuring. Bake until the tops spring back at the touch of your finger and a toothpick inserted into the center comes out clean.
8. *Remove from* tins and cool completely before filling and icing.

Finishing Touches: Ice with Caramel Buttercream (119) and garnish with Dark Chocolate Ganache (126), Caramel Filling (126), and Toasted Coconut (127).

Chocolate Peppermint Cupcakes

wet ingredients

- ½ cup dark chocolate chopped into small pieces
- ½ cup boiling water
- ½ cup sour cream
- ½ cup unsweetened applesauce
- ½ cup vegetable oil
- 3 large eggs
- 1 Tbsp. pure vanilla
- 1 tsp. peppermint extract

dry ingredients

- 1½ cups all-purpose flour
- 1 cup granulated sugar
- 1 Tbsp. baking powder
- ½ tsp. salt
- ½ cup Dutch-processed cocoa powder

Preparation

1. Preheat oven to 350 degrees.
2. Place chocolate in the bowl of a stand mixer. Pour boiling water over chocolate and let sit for 1 minute. Using the whisk attachment, mix until smooth. Scrape down the sides of the bowl.
3. Add sour cream, applesauce, oil, eggs, vanilla, and peppermint extract.
4. In a separate bowl, sift flour, sugar, baking powder, salt, and cocoa powder.
5. Turn the stand mixer on low and add dry ingredients and mix until just incorporated. Batter should be smooth.
6. Line two standard muffin tins with paper cupcake liners. Fill each cup two-thirds full with batter. Use an ice cream scoop for perfect measuring. Bake until the tops spring back at the touch of your finger and a toothpick inserted into the center comes out clean.
7. Remove from tins and cool completely before filling and icing.

Finishing Touches: Apply a single layer of Dark Chocolate Ganache (126), ice with Peppermint Buttercream (119), and garnish with chocolate or peppermint bark.

Janell Brown

Butter Toffee Crunch Cupcakes

This cupcake is filled with English butter toffee, iced in vanilla buttercream, and rolled in more toffee. It has a warm chocolate butter flavor and a slight crunch.

wet ingredients

½ cup dark chocolate chopped into small pieces
½ cup boiling water
½ cup sour cream
½ cup unsweetened applesauce
½ cup vegetable oil
3 large eggs
1 Tbsp. pure vanilla

dry ingredients

1½ cups all-purpose flour
1 cup granulated sugar
1 Tbsp. baking powder
½ tsp. salt
½ cup Dutch-processed cocoa powder
½ cup crushed English butter toffee

Preparation

1. *Preheat oven* to 350 degrees.

2. *Place chocolate* in the bowl of a stand mixer. Pour boiling water over chocolate and let sit for 1 minute. Using the whisk attachment, mix until smooth. Scrape down the sides of the bowl.

3. *Add sour* cream, applesauce, oil, eggs, and vanilla.

4. *In a* separate bowl, sift flour, sugar, baking powder, salt, and cocoa powder.

5. *Turn the* stand mixer on low and add dry ingredients and mix until just incorporated. Batter should be smooth.

6. *Fold in* English toffee.

7. *Line two* standard muffin tins with paper cupcake liners. Fill each cup two-thirds full with batter. Use an ice cream scoop for perfect measuring. Bake until the tops spring back at the touch of your finger and a toothpick inserted into the center comes out clean.

8. *Remove from* tins and cool completely before filling and icing.

Finishing Touches: Ice with Caramel Buttercream (119) and roll top of cupcake in crushed English butter toffee.

The Dark Side

S'mores Cupcakes

wet ingredients

½ cup dark chocolate chopped into
    small pieces
½ cup boiling water
½ cup sour cream
½ cup unsweetened applesauce
½ cup vegetable oil
3 large eggs
1 Tbsp. pure vanilla

dry ingredients

1½ cups all-purpose flour
1 cup granulated sugar
1 Tbsp. baking powder
½ tsp. salt
½ cup Dutch-processed cocoa
    powder

Preparation

1. *Preheat oven* to 350 degrees.

2. *Place chocolate* in the bowl of a stand mixer. Pour boiling water over chocolate and let sit for 1 minute. Using the whisk attachment, mix until smooth. Scrape down the sides of the bowl.

3. *Add sour* cream, applesauce, oil, eggs, and vanilla.

4. *In a* separate bowl, sift flour, sugar, baking powder, salt, and cocoa powder.

5. *Turn the* stand mixer on low and add dry ingredients and mix until just incorporated. Batter should be smooth.

6. *Line two* standard muffin tins with paper cupcake liners. Fill each cup two-thirds full with batter. Use an ice cream scoop for perfect measuring. Bake until the tops spring back at the touch of your finger and a toothpick inserted into the center comes out clean.

7. *Remove from* tins and cool completely before filling and icing.

Finishing Touches: Ice with Marshmallow Icing (117). Roll sides of cupcakes in crushed graham crackers. Lightly brown top of cupcakes with a kitchen blow torch and top with mini marshmallows and chocolate squares.

Janell Brown

Warm & Comforting

Mayan Hot Chocolate Cupcakes

This cupcake is a winter favorite. The cinnamon gives these chocolate cupcakes a little kick! All you need is a warm fire and a glass of cold milk to make this treat complete.

wet ingredients

- ½ cup dark chocolate chopped into small pieces
- ½ cup boiling water
- ½ cup sour cream
- ½ cup unsweetened applesauce
- ½ cup vegetable oil
- 3 large eggs
- 1 Tbsp. pure vanilla

dry ingredients

- 1½ cups all-purpose flour
- 1 cup granulated sugar
- 1 Tbsp. baking powder
- ½ tsp. salt
- ½ cup Dutch-processed cocoa powder
- 1 Tbsp. ground cinnamon

Preparation

1. *Preheat oven* to 350 degrees.
2. *Place chocolate* in the bowl of a stand mixer. Pour boiling water over chocolate and let sit for 1 minute. Using the whisk attachment, mix until smooth. Scrape down the sides of the bowl.
3. *Add sour* cream, applesauce, oil, eggs, and vanilla.
4. *In a* separate bowl, sift flour, sugar, baking powder, salt, cocoa, and cinnamon.
5. *Turn the* stand mixer on low and add dry ingredients and mix until just incorporated. Batter should be smooth.
6. *Line two* standard muffin tins with paper cupcake liners. Fill each cup two-thirds full with batter. Use an ice cream scoop for perfect measuring. Bake until the tops spring back at the touch of your finger and a toothpick inserted into the center comes out clean.
7. *Remove from* tins and cool completely before filling and icing.

Finishing Touches: Ice with Cinnamon Buttercream (120) and garnish with cinnamon and sugar.

NOTE: To create a "hot chocolate" look, add a pirouette cookie, cinnamon stick, or straw for garnish.

Warm & Comforting

79

Snickerdoodle Cupcakes

Like the cookie, this cupcake has a crisp outer shell and a swirl of cinnamon and sugar that will take you back to warm cookies and cold milk on a Sunday afternoon.

wet ingredients

¼ cup unsalted butter, softened
½ cup sour cream
¼ cup buttermilk
¼ cup unsweetened applesauce
½ cup vegetable oil
3 large eggs
2 Tbsp. pure vanilla
1 Tbsp. vanilla bean paste

dry ingredients

1 cup granulated sugar
2 cups all-purpose flour
1¼ Tbsp. baking powder
½ tsp. salt
3 Tbsp. cinnamon
2 Tbsp. granulated sugar

Preparation

1. *Preheat oven* to 350 degrees.

2. *Beat butter* and 1 cup sugar in the bowl of a stand mixer with the paddle attachment on medium speed until smooth. Stop mixer and scrape down the sides of the bowl. Add sour cream, buttermilk, applesauce, oil, eggs, vanilla, and vanilla bean paste. Mix until ingredients are well blended and smooth.

3. *In a* separate bowl, sift flour, baking powder, and salt.

4. *Mix cinnamon* and remaining sugar together.

5. *Turn the* stand mixer on low and add dry ingredients from step three until just incorporated. The batter should be smooth.

6. *Add cinnamon* and sugar mixture and swirl into batter.

7. *Line two* standard muffin tins with paper cupcake liners. Fill each cup two-thirds full with batter. Use an ice cream scoop for perfect measuring. Bake until the tops spring back at the touch of your finger and the edges are just golden brown, 20–25 minutes.

8. *Remove from* tins and cool completely before filling or icing.

Finishing Touches:. Ice with Cream Cheese Icing (120) and garnish with cinnamon and sugar.

NOTE: Bake this cupcake until the top is a golden brown. This will give the outer shell a nice crunch, just like the cookie.

Janell Brown

Horchata Cupcakes

MAKES 24 Standard-Size Cupcakes

This cupcake is gluten-free and has the taste of the favorite Mexican drink horchata. It calls for rice milk and cinnamon to create the perfect blend of sugar and spice.

wet ingredients

- ¼ cup unsalted butter, softened
- ½ cup sour cream
- ¼ cup horchata (spiced rice milk)
- ¼ cup unsweetened applesauce
- ½ cup vegetable oil
- 3 large eggs
- 2 Tbsp. pure vanilla
- 1 Tbsp. vanilla bean paste

dry ingredients

- 1 cup granulated sugar
- 2 cups rice flour
- 1¼ Tbsp. baking powder
- ½ tsp. salt

Preparation

1. *Preheat the* oven to 350 degrees.

2. *Beat butter* and sugar in the bowl of a stand mixer with the paddle attachment on medium speed until smooth. Stop mixer and scrape down the sides of the bowl. Add sour cream, horchata, applesauce, oil, eggs, vanilla, and vanilla bean paste. Mix until ingredients are well blended and smooth.

3. *In a* separate bowl sift rice flour, baking powder, and salt.

4. *Turn the* stand mixer on low and add dry ingredients until just incorporated. The batter should be smooth.

5. *Line two* standard muffin tins with paper cupcake liners. Fill each cup two-thirds full with batter. Use an ice cream scoop for perfect measuring. Bake until the tops spring back at the touch of your finger and the edges are just golden brown, 20–25 minutes.

6. *Remove from* tins and cool completely before filling or icing.

Finishing Touches: Ice with Whipped Mascarpone Icing (122) and garnish with cinnamon and sugar.

NOTE: Use cinnamon and sugar–covered puffed rice for a garnish to keep this cupcake completely gluten-free. If gluten-free is not necessary, you can top with a piece of churro!

Warm & Comforting

Carrot Ginger Cupcakes

wet ingredients

3 large eggs
1½ cup vegetable oil
¼ cup orange juice
¼ cup sour cream
¼ cup unsweetened applesauce
¼ cup buttermilk
1 tsp. vanilla extract
3 large carrots, peeled and grated
½ cup raisins

dry ingredients

2 cups sugar
3 cups all-purpose flour
2 tsp. baking powder
1 tsp. baking soda
¾ tsp. ground cinnamon
1 tsp. salt
1 Tbsp. peeled, grated fresh ginger

Preparation

1. *Preheat oven* to 350 degrees.
2. *Beat eggs,* sugar, oil, orange juice, sour cream, applesauce, buttermilk, and vanilla in the bowl of a stand mixer with the paddle attachment on medium speed until smooth. Stop mixer and scrape down the sides of the bowl.
3. *In a* separate bowl, sift flour, baking powder, baking soda, cinnamon, salt, and ginger.
4. *Turn the* stand mixer on low and add dry ingredients until just incorporated. The batter should be smooth.
5. *Fold carrots* and raisins into batter until smooth.
6. *Line two* standard muffin tins with paper cupcake liners. Fill each cup two-thirds full with batter. Use an ice cream scoop for perfect measuring. Bake until the tops spring back at the touch of your finger and the edges are just golden brown, 20–25 minutes.
7. *Remove from* tins and cool completely before icing.

Finishing Touches: Ice with Cream Cheese Icing (120) and garnish with a dash of cinnamon and walnuts.

Note: You can customize this recipe to fit your taste buds. If you are not a raisin fan, or if you want to add nuts, feel free to omit or add to your taste.

Janell Brown

Pumpkin Chocolate Chip Cupcakes

This cupcake is a delicious version of the pumpkin chocolate chip cookie. When topped with fluffy cream cheese icing, this cupcake is sure to be devoured by all.

MAKES
24
Standard-Size Cupcakes

wet ingredients

- ¼ cup unsalted butter, softened
- ½ cup sour cream
- ¼ cup buttermilk
- ¼ cup unsweetened applesauce
- ½ cup vegetable oil
- 3 large eggs
- 2 Tbsp. pure vanilla
- 1 (16-oz.) can pumpkin

dry ingredients

- ½ cup granulated sugar
- 2 cups all-purpose flour
- 2 tsp. ground cinnamon
- ½ tsp. ginger
- ⅛ tsp. nutmeg
- 1¼ Tbsp. baking powder
- ½ tsp. salt
- ½ cup + 2 Tbsp. packed brown sugar

Preparation

1. *Preheat oven* to 350 degrees.

2. *Beat butter* and granulated sugar in the bowl of a stand mixer with the paddle attachment on medium speed until smooth. Stop mixer and scrape down the sides of the bowl. Add sour cream, buttermilk, applesauce, oil, eggs, vanilla, and canned pumpkin. Mix until ingredients are well blended and smooth.

3. *In a* separate bowl, sift flour, spices, baking powder, salt, and brown sugar.

4. *Turn the* stand mixer on low and add dry ingredients until just incorporated. The batter should be smooth.

5. *Line two* standard muffin tins with paper cupcake liners. Fill each cup two-thirds full with batter. Use an ice cream scoop for perfect measuring. Bake until the tops spring back at the touch of your finger and the edges are just golden brown, 20–25 minutes.

6. *Remove from* tins and cool completely before icing.

Finishing Touches: Dip the tops of cupcakes in Dark Chocolate Ganache (126), ice with Cream Cheese Icing (120), and garnish with mini chocolate chips and Perfect Pumpkins (155).

Warm & Comforting

Eggnog Cupcakes

The smell of this cupcake baking brings the feel of Christmas to the kitchen. The icing is so delicious you will want to garnish it with a straw. With these cupcakes you can have the taste and smell of Christmas year round.

wet ingredients

¼ cup unsalted butter, softened
½ cup sour cream
¼ cup eggnog
¼ cup unsweetened applesauce
½ cup vegetable oil
3 large eggs
2 Tbsp. pure vanilla
1 Tbsp. rum extract
1 Tbsp. vanilla bean paste

dry ingredients

1 cup granulated sugar
2 cups all-purpose flour
1¼ Tbsp. baking powder
¼ tsp. nutmeg
½ tsp. salt

Preparation

1. *Preheat oven* to 350 degrees.

2. *Beat butter* and sugar in the bowl of a stand mixer with the paddle attachment on medium speed until smooth. Stop mixer and scrape down the sides of the bowl. Add sour cream, eggnog, applesauce, oil, eggs, vanilla, rum extract, and vanilla bean paste. Mix until ingredients are well blended and smooth.

3. *In a* separate bowl, sift flour, baking powder, nutmeg, and salt.

4. *Turn the* stand mixer on low and add dry ingredients until just incorporated. The batter should be smooth.

5. *Line two* standard muffin tins with paper cupcake liners. Fill each cup two-thirds full with batter. Use an ice cream scoop for perfect measuring. Bake until the tops spring back at the touch of your finger and the edges are just golden brown, 20–25 minutes.

6. *Remove from* tins and cool completely before filling or icing.

Finishing Touches: Ice with Eggnog Buttercream (120), and add a cinnamon stick for garnish.

NOTE: This is a nonalcoholic version of an eggnog cupcake.

Janell Brown

Apple Crisp Cupcakes

This cupcake is best when warm and served with a scoop of vanilla bean ice cream. You can eat it un-iced with the streusel topping, or layer it with smooth vanilla buttercream. Either way, it's an American classic that you will want to bake time and time again.

wet ingredients

- ¼ cup unsalted butter, softened
- ½ cup sour cream
- ¼ cup buttermilk
- ¼ cup unsweetened applesauce
- ½ cup vegetable oil
- 3 large eggs
- 2 Tbsp. pure vanilla
- 1 Tbsp. vanilla bean paste
- 1 cup canned apple pie filling

dry ingredients

- 1 cup granulated sugar
- 2 cups all-purpose flour
- 1¼ Tbsp. baking powder
- 1 tsp. cinnamon
- 1 tsp. allspice
- ½ tsp. salt
- Streusel Topping (128)

Preparation

1. *Preheat oven* to 350 degrees.
2. *Beat butter* and sugar in the bowl of a stand mixer with the paddle attachment on medium speed until smooth. Stop mixer and scrape down the sides of the bowl. Add sour cream, buttermilk, applesauce, oil, eggs, vanilla, vanilla bean paste, and apple pie filling. Mix until ingredients are well blended and smooth.
3. *In a* separate bowl sift flour, baking powder, spices, and salt.
4. *Turn the* stand mixer on low and add dry ingredients until just incorporated. The batter should be smooth.
5. *Line two* standard muffin tins with paper cupcake liners. Fill each cup two-thirds full with batter. Use an ice cream scoop for perfect measuring.
6. *Sprinkle streusel* topping over the top of each unbaked cupcake.
7. *Bake until* the edges are just golden brown, 20–25 minutes.
8. *Remove from* tins and cool slightly.

Finishing Touches: Top cupcakes with scoops of vanilla bean ice cream and a caramel drizzle, or ice them with Vanilla Buttercream (118).

Warm & Comforting

Sweet Potato Cupcakes

This is the perfect cupcake to serve after a Thanksgiving dinner or Christmas party. The tender mash of the sweet potato makes this cupcake moist, colorful, and full of flavor.

wet ingredients

¼ cup unsalted butter, softened
½ cup sour cream
¼ cup buttermilk
¼ cup unsweetened applesauce
½ cup vegetable oil
3 large eggs
2 Tbsp. pure vanilla
1 (16-oz.) can sweet potatoes

dry ingredients

½ cup granulated sugar
2 cups all-purpose flour
2 tsp. ground cinnamon
½ tsp. ginger
⅛ tsp. nutmeg
½ cup + 2 Tbsp. packed brown sugar
1¼ Tbsp. baking powder
½ tsp. salt

Preparation

1. *Preheat oven* to 350 degrees.

2. *Beat butter* and granulated sugar in the bowl of a stand mixer with the paddle attachment on medium speed until smooth. Stop mixer and scrape down the sides of the bowl. Add sour cream, buttermilk, applesauce, oil, eggs, vanilla, and canned sweet potato. Mix until ingredients are well blended and smooth.

3. *In a* separate bowl, sift flour, spices, brown sugar, baking powder, and salt.

4. *Turn the* stand mixer on low and add dry ingredients until just incorporated. The batter should be smooth.

5. *Line two* standard muffin tins with paper cupcake liners. Fill each cup two-thirds full with batter. Use an ice cream scoop for perfect measuring. Bake until the tops spring back at the touch of your finger and the edges are just golden brown, 20–25 minutes.

6. *Remove from* tins and cool completely before filling or icing.

Finishing Touches: Ice with Maple Buttercream (120) and top with brown sugar and marshmallows.

Janell Brown

Maple Brown Sugar Cupcakes

Also known as the Luke Skywalker Cupcake, *this flavor combination helped us win the second round of the Star Wars episode of* Cupcake Wars. *The sweet maple brown sugar cake combined with the salty peanut butter cream cheese reminds me of putting peanut butter on my pancakes when I was a kid.*

wet ingredients

¼ cup unsalted butter, softened

½ cup sour cream

¼ cup buttermilk

¼ cup unsweetened applesauce

½ cup vegetable oil

3 large eggs

2 Tbsp. pure vanilla

1 Tbsp. maple extract

dry ingredients

1 cup granulated sugar

2 cups all-purpose flour

⅓ cup packed brown sugar

1¼ Tbsp. baking powder

½ tsp. salt

Preparation

1. *Preheat the* oven to 350 degrees.

2. *Beat butter* and sugar in the bowl of a stand mixer with the paddle attachment on medium speed until smooth. Stop mixer and scrape down the sides of the bowl. Add sour cream, buttermilk, applesauce, oil, eggs, vanilla, and maple extract. Mix until ingredients are well blended and smooth.

3. *In a* separate bowl sift flour, brown sugar, baking powder, and salt.

4. *Turn the* stand mixer on low and add dry ingredients until just incorporated. The batter should be smooth.

5. *Line two* standard muffin tins with paper cupcake liners. Fill each cup two-thirds full with batter. Use an ice cream scoop for perfect measuring. Bake until the tops spring back at the touch of your finger and the edges are just golden brown, 20–25 minutes.

6. *Remove from* tins and cool completely before filling or icing.

Finishing Touches: Ice with Peanut Butter Cream (118) and Peanut Butter Cream Cheese (121). Garnish with real maple syrup, brown sugar, and crushed peanuts.

Warm & Comforting

A Little Nutty

Butter Almond Poppy Seed Cupcakes

The extract of almonds and flecks of poppy seed enhance the buttery flavor of this cupcake. It is best when served with a light sugar glaze and slivered almonds.

wet ingredients

- ½ cup unsalted butter, softened
- ½ cup sour cream
- ¼ cup buttermilk
- ¼ cup unsweetened applesauce
- ½ cup vegetable oil
- 3 large eggs
- 2 Tbsp. pure vanilla
- 1 Tbsp. almond extract

dry ingredients

- 1 cup granulated sugar
- 2 cups all-purpose flour
- 1¼ Tbsp. baking powder
- 2 Tbsp. poppy seeds
- ½ tsp. salt

Preparation

1. *Preheat the* oven to 350 degrees.
2. *Beat butter* and sugar in the bowl of a stand mixer with the paddle attachment on medium speed until smooth. Stop mixer and scrape down the sides of the bowl. Add sour cream, buttermilk, applesauce, oil, eggs, vanilla, and almond extract. Mix until ingredients are well blended and smooth.
3. *In a* separate bowl, sift flour, baking powder, poppy seeds, and salt.
4. *Turn the* stand mixer on low and add dry ingredients until just incorporated. The batter should be smooth.
5. *Line two* standard muffin tins with paper cupcake liners. Fill each cup two-thirds full with batter. Use an ice cream scoop for perfect measuring. Bake until the tops spring back at the touch of your finger and the edges are just golden brown, 15–20 minutes.
6. *Remove from* tins and cool completely before filling or icing.

Finishing Touches: Ice with Vanilla Buttercream (118) and garnish with poppy seeds and almond slivers.

NOTE: The extra butter in this cupcake will cause it to brown quickly when baking. Make sure the center is completely cooked before removing from the oven.

Pistachio Cream Cupcakes

wet ingredients

¼ cup unsalted butter, softened
½ cup sour cream
¼ cup buttermilk
¼ cup unsweetened applesauce
½ cup vegetable oil
3 large eggs
2 Tbsp. pure vanilla
green food coloring

dry ingredients

1 cup granulated sugar
¼ cup pistachio pudding mix
2 cups all-purpose flour
1¼ Tbsp. baking powder
½ tsp. salt
¾ cup shelled and crushed pistachios

Preparation

1. *Preheat the* oven to 350 degrees.

2. *Beat butter* and sugar in the bowl of a stand mixer with the paddle attachment on medium speed until smooth. Stop mixer and scrape down the sides of the bowl. Add sour cream, buttermilk, applesauce, oil, eggs, and vanilla. Mix until ingredients are well blended and smooth.

3. *In a* separate bowl, sift pistachio pudding mix, flour, baking powder, and salt.

4. *Turn the* stand mixer on low and add dry ingredients until just incorporated. The batter should be smooth.

5. *Add one* drop of green food coloring and mix well.

6. *Fold in* shelled and crushed pistachios.

7. *Line two* standard muffin tins with paper cupcake liners. Fill each cup two-thirds full with batter. Use an ice cream scoop for perfect measuring. Bake until the tops spring back at the touch of your finger and the edges are just golden brown, 20–25 minutes.

8. *Remove from* tins and cool completely before filling or icing.

Finishing Touches: Ice with Pistachio Buttercream (120) and top with crushed pistachios.

NOTE: Don't add too much food coloring to the batter. If too much is added, the cake will look artificial and unappetizing.

Janell Brown

Peanut Butter and Jelly Cupcakes

MAKES
24
Standard-Size Cupcakes

wet ingredients

¼ cup unsalted butter, softened
²⁄₃ cup natural creamy peanut butter
½ cup sour cream
¼ cup buttermilk
¼ cup unsweetened applesauce
½ cup vegetable oil
3 large eggs
2 Tbsp. pure vanilla

dry ingredients

1 cup granulated sugar
¼ cup instant vanilla pudding mix
2 cups all-purpose flour
1¼ Tbsp. baking powder
½ tsp. salt

Preparation

1. *Preheat oven* to 350 degrees.

2. *Beat butter,* peanut butter, and sugar in the bowl of a stand mixer with the paddle attachment on medium speed until smooth. Stop mixer and scrape down the sides of the bowl. Add sour cream, buttermilk, applesauce, oil, eggs, and vanilla. Mix until ingredients are well blended and smooth.

3. *In a* separate bowl, sift dry vanilla pudding, flour, baking powder, and salt.

4. *Turn the* stand mixer on low and add dry ingredients until just incorporated. The batter should be smooth.

5. *Line two* standard muffin tins with paper cupcake liners. Fill each cup two-thirds full with batter. Use an ice cream scoop for perfect measuring. Bake until the tops spring back at the touch of your finger and the edges are just golden brown, 20–25 minutes.

6. *Remove from* tins and cool completely before filling or icing.

Finishing Touches: Core cupcakes and fill with Raspberry Puree (128) and ice with Peanut Butter Cream Cheese (121). Garnish with a dollop of raspberry jam and a Nutter Butter or peanuts.

NOTE: Be sure to fill these cupcakes with either a raspberry or strawberry puree to have the full PB&J effect!

A Little Nutty

Caramel Pecan Cupcakes

This is a twist on a southern favorite—caramel pecan pie. This cupcake is loaded with pecans, filled with caramel, and topped with a cream cheese icing, caramel drizzle, and candied pecans.

wet ingredients

¼ cup unsalted butter, softened
½ cup sour cream
¼ cup buttermilk
¼ cup unsweetened applesauce
½ cup vegetable oil
3 large eggs
2 Tbsp. pure vanilla
1 Tbsp. vanilla bean paste

dry ingredients

1 cup granulated sugar
¼ cup vanilla instant dry pudding mix
2 cups all-purpose flour
1 ¼ Tbsp. baking powder
½ tsp. salt
½ cup crushed pecans

Preparation

1. *Preheat oven* to 350 degrees.

2. *Beat butter* and sugar in the bowl of a stand mixer with the paddle attachment on medium speed until smooth. Stop mixer and scrape down the sides of the bowl. Add sour cream, buttermilk, applesauce, oil, eggs, vanilla, and vanilla bean paste. Mix until ingredients are well blended and smooth.

3. *In a* separate bowl, sift dry vanilla pudding, flour, baking powder, and salt.

4. *Turn the* stand mixer on low and add dry ingredients. Mix until just incorporated. The batter should be smooth. Fold in crushed pecans.

5. *Line two* standard muffin tins with paper cupcake liners. Fill each cup two-thirds full with batter. Use an ice cream scoop for perfect measuring. Bake until the tops spring back at the touch of your finger and the edges are just golden brown, 20–25 minutes.

6. *Remove from* tins and cool completely before filling or icing.

Finishing Touches: Core center of cupcake and fill with Caramel Filling (126). Ice with Cream Cheese Icing (120), drizzle with caramel, and top with crushed pecans.

Janell Brown

Rocky Road Cupcakes

If life gives you a "rocky road," eating this cupcake will make it better! Chocolate, almonds, and marshmallows come together to form a moist, gooey cupcake with a crunch.

wet ingredients

½ cup dark chocolate chopped into small pieces
½ cup boiling water
½ cup sour cream
½ cup unsweetened applesauce
½ cup vegetable oil
3 large eggs
1 Tbsp. almond extract
1 Tbsp. pure vanilla

dry ingredients

1½ cups all-purpose flour
1 cup granulated sugar
1 Tbsp. baking powder
½ tsp. salt
½ cup Dutch-processed cocoa powder
1 cup mini marshmallows
½ cup crushed almonds

Preparation

1. *Preheat oven* to 350 degrees.
2. *Place chocolate* in the bowl of a stand mixer.

Pour boiling water over chocolate and let sit for 1 minute. Using the whisk attachment, mix until smooth. Scrape down the sides of the bowl.

3. *Add sour* cream, applesauce, oil, eggs, almond extract, and vanilla.

4. *In a* separate bowl sift flour, sugar, baking powder, salt, and cocoa powder.

5. *Turn the* stand mixer on low and add dry ingredients. Mix until just incorporated. Batter should be smooth.

6. *Fold mini* marshmallows and crushed almonds into batter.

7. *Line two* standard muffin tins with paper cupcake liners. Fill each cup two-thirds full with batter. Use an ice cream scoop for perfect measuring. Bake until the tops spring back at the touch of your finger and a toothpick inserted into the center comes out clean.

8. *Remove from* tins and cool completely before filling and icing.

Finishing Touches: Core center of cupcake and fill with marshmallow creme. Ice with Chocolate Buttercream (118) and garnish with mini marshmallows and crushed almonds.

German Chocolate Cupcakes

Warm German chocolate icing is what makes this cupcake famous. These cupcakes will not stay on the plate for long.

wet ingredients

- ½ cup dark chocolate chopped into small pieces
- ½ cup boiling water
- ½ cup sour cream
- ½ cup unsweetened applesauce
- ½ cup vegetable oil
- 3 large eggs
- 1 Tbsp. pure vanilla

dry ingredients

- 1½ cups all-purpose flour
- 1 cup granulated sugar
- 1 Tbsp. baking powder
- ½ tsp. salt
- ½ cup Dutch-processed cocoa powder

Preparation

1. Preheat oven to 350 degrees.

2. Place chocolate in the bowl of a stand mixer. Pour boiling water over chocolate and let sit for 1 minute. Using the whisk attachment, mix until smooth. Scrape down the sides of the bowl.

3. Add sour cream, applesauce, oil, eggs, and vanilla.

4. In a separate bowl, sift flour, sugar, baking powder, salt, and cocoa powder.

5. Turn the stand mixer on low and add dry ingredients and mix until just incorporated. Batter should be smooth.

6. Line two standard muffin tins with paper cupcake liners. Fill each cup two-thirds full with batter. Use an ice cream scoop for perfect measuring. Bake until the tops spring back at the touch of your finger and a toothpick inserted into the center comes out clean.

7. Remove from tins and cool completely before icing.

Finishing Touches: **Prepare** German Chocolate Icing (122) and scoop with a fork and spread onto tops of cupcakes. Top with pecans and drizzle with Dark Chocolate Ganache (126).

Almond Joy Cupcakes

MAKES 24 Standard-Size Cupcakes

Like the name, this cupcake will bring happiness and joy to all who bite into it. Chocolate, almond, coconut cake iced with a layer of coconut cream cheese and garnished with shredded coconut and a single almond make this cupcake irresistible.

wet ingredients

- ½ cup dark chocolate chopped into small pieces
- ½ cup boiling water
- ½ cup sour cream
- ½ cup unsweetened applesauce
- ½ cup vegetable oil
- 3 large eggs
- 1½ tsp. almond extract
- 1 Tbsp. pure vanilla
- ½ cup shredded coconut

dry ingredients

- 1½ cups all-purpose flour
- 1 cup granulated sugar
- 1 Tbsp. baking powder
- ½ tsp. salt
- ½ cup Dutch-processed cocoa powder

Preparation

1. Preheat oven to 350 degrees.

2. Place chocolate in the bowl of a stand mixer. Pour boiling water over chocolate and let sit for 1 minute. Using the whisk attachment, mix until smooth. Scrape down the sides of the bowl.

3. Add sour cream, applesauce, oil, eggs, almond extract, and vanilla.

4. In a separate bowl, sift flour, sugar, baking powder, salt, and cocoa powder.

5. Turn the stand mixer on low and add dry ingredients. Mix until just incorporated. Batter should be smooth.

6. Fold shredded coconut into batter.

7. Line two standard muffin tins with paper cupcake liners. Fill each cup two-thirds full with batter. Use an ice cream scoop for perfect measuring. Bake until the tops spring back at the touch of your finger and a toothpick inserted into the center comes out clean.

8. Remove from tins and cool completely before filling and icing.

Finishing Touches: Ice with Coconut Cream Cheese (121) and garnish with shredded coconut and a single almond.

A Little Nutty

Nutella Cupcakes

Chocolate and hazelnut come together to create a rich, moist, and unforgettable cupcake. One of my personal favorites, you will be wanting more after each bite.

Janell Brown

wet ingredients

½ cup dark chocolate chopped into small pieces
½ cup boiling water
½ cup sour cream
½ cup unsweetened applesauce
½ cup vegetable oil
3 large eggs
1 Tbsp. pure vanilla
½ cup Nutella

dry ingredients

1½ cups all-purpose flour
1 cup granulated sugar
1 Tbsp. baking powder
½ tsp. salt
½ cup Dutch-processed cocoa powder

Preparation

1. *Preheat oven* to 350 degrees.
2. *Place chocolate* in the bowl of a stand mixer. Pour boiling water over chocolate and let sit for 1 minute. Using the whisk attachment, mix until smooth. Scrape down the sides of the bowl.
3. *Add sour* cream, applesauce, oil, eggs, and vanilla.
4. *In a* separate bowl, sift flour, sugar, baking powder, salt, and cocoa powder.
5. *Turn the* stand mixer on low and add dry ingredients. Mix until just incorporated. Batter should be smooth.
6. *Stir Nutella* into chocolate batter until fully blended.
7. *Line two* standard muffin tins with paper cupcake liners. Fill each cup two-thirds full with batter. Use an ice cream scoop for perfect measuring. Bake until the tops spring back at the touch of your finger and a toothpick inserted into the center comes out clean.
8. *Remove from* tins and cool completely before filling and icing.

Finishing Touches: Ice by adding a thick layer of Nutella followed by Chocolate Buttercream (118) and chopped hazelnuts on top.

Icings

Icing Basics

The best part of any cupcake is the "icing on the cake." Selecting and preparing the right icing to complement the flavor of the cupcake is vital. Understanding the purpose and use for each icing will help you create the perfect cupcake. American buttercreams are sweet and simple and use powdered sugar for the icing base. This is the icing most people are familiar with and imagine tasting when biting into a birthday cupcake. Cream cheese icing is also made with a powdered sugar base but is more tangy than sweet—a flavor provided by the rich blocks of cream cheese that are creamed together with butter, sugar, and vanilla. Adding a small amount of water to powdered sugar creates a glaze. On a cupcake, a glaze is sweet but not overbearing. For the cupcake lover who always complains that there is too much icing on their cupcake, a glaze is a great alternative. European icings such as French buttercream, Italian meringue, or Swiss meringue are made using an egg or meringue base for the icing. They are more time consuming and less sweet but create a light and fluffy texture and flavor that can't be obtained any other way. The technique for creating each icing is different, so read and follow the directions to ensure that your icing takes the cake. (For icing and decorating tools, see page 8.)

Marshmallow Icing

¾ cup granulated sugar
½ cup light corn syrup
¼ cup water
⅛ tsp. salt
2 large egg whites
¼ tsp. cream of tartar
1½ tsp. vanilla extract

Instructions:

Stir together sugar, corn syrup, water, and salt in a small saucepan over high heat. Bring to a boil, stirring occasionally, until the mixture reaches 240 degrees on a candy thermometer.

While the syrup is cooking, place egg whites and cream of tartar in the bowl of a stand mixer fitted with the whisk attachment. Whip until soft peaks start to form.

When the syrup reaches 240 degrees, reduce the mixer speed to low and slowly drizzle the syrup into the whipped egg whites. Increase the speed and whip until the marshmallow icing is stiff and glossy, about 7 minutes. Add vanilla and whip 2 more minutes. Use immediately.

Citrus Glaze

¼ tsp. grated zest
4 Tbsp. citrus juice
1½–2 cups powdered sugar

Instructions:

Add zest to citrus juice and pour over powdered sugar. Whisk together until smooth and the glaze is thick but pourable. Use immediately.

Fresh Whipped Cream

2 cups heavy cream
¼ cup powdered sugar

Instructions:

Whisk cream until soft peaks begin to form. Do not overmix. Add powdered sugar and whisk until combined. Use immediately.

Peanut Butter Cream

½ cup unsalted butter, melted
½ cup powdered sugar
1 cup smooth peanut butter
¼ tsp. salt
1 tsp. vanilla extract

Instructions:

Mix all ingredients together until smooth. Use immediately.

White Chocolate Buttercream

1 cup butter, softened
2–2½ cups powdered sugar, divided
8 oz. white chocolate, melted and cooled
4 Tbsp. heavy cream

Instructions:

In a large bowl, beat butter and 2 cups powdered sugar at low speed until light and fluffy. Slowly pour in melted and cooled white chocolate and heavy cream.

Beat on high for 3 minutes, making sure to scrape the sides of the bowl.

Add remaining powdered sugar, if desired, and beat until smooth.

Chocolate Buttercream

Instructions:

Add 1½ cups cocoa powder and ¼ cup Dark Chocolate Ganache (126) to one batch of Vanilla Buttercream (above).

Vanilla Buttercream

2 lbs. butter, softened
4 lbs. powdered sugar, divided
¼ milk
3 Tbsp. vanilla
pinch of salt

Instructions:

In a stand mixer bowl with the paddle attachment, beat butter until light, completely smooth, and fluffy. Turn the mixer speed to low and add half of the powdered sugar. Mix until smooth. Alternately, add remaining powdered sugar and milk until smooth and creamy. Add vanilla and salt. Beat until smooth.

Raspberry Buttercream

Instructions:

Add ¼ cup Raspberry Puree (128) to Vanilla Buttercream (118) and beat until smooth. Add 1 cup powdered sugar if needed to thicken.

Strawberry Buttercream

Instructions:

Add ¼ cup Strawberry Puree (128) to Vanilla Buttercream (118) and beat until smooth. Add 1 cup powdered sugar if needed to thicken.

Grasshopper Buttercream

Instructions:

Add 2 teaspoons mint extract and 1 drop green food coloring to a batch of Vanilla Buttercream (118) and beat until incorporated. Fold in ¼ cup crushed Oreos.

Caramel Buttercream

Instructions:

Add 3 teaspoons caramel extract and 2 tablespoons caramel sauce to a batch of Vanilla Buttercream (118). Beat until smooth.

Blackberry Buttercream

Instructions:

Add ¼ cup Blackberry Puree (128) to Vanilla Buttercream (118) and beat until smooth. Add 1 cup powdered sugar if needed to thicken.

Peppermint Buttercream

Instructions:

Add ¼ cup crushed peppermint to a batch of Vanilla Buttercream (118) and fold in until smooth.

Cinnamon Buttercream

Instructions:

Mix 1 tablespoon cinnamon and 2 tablespoons sugar in a small bowl. Add 2 tablespoons of the cinnamon and sugar mixture to a batch of Vanilla Buttercream (118). Beat until smooth.

Maple Buttercream

Instructions:

Mix 2–3 teaspoons maple extract and 2 tablespoons real maple syrup into one batch of Vanilla Buttercream (118). Beat until smooth.

Pistachio Buttercream

Instructions:

Add 1 small pouch of pistachio pudding mix and 2 tablespoons milk to a batch of Vanilla Buttercream (118). Mix until smooth.

Eggnog Buttercream

Instructions:

Mix 2–3 teaspoons rum extract and ¼ teaspoon nutmeg into a batch of Vanilla Buttercream (118). Beat until smooth. More extract may be added until desired flavor is reached.

Cream Cheese Icing

8 oz. butter, softened
16 oz. cream cheese, softened
2 lbs. powdered sugar
½ tsp. vanilla

Instructions:

In a stand mixer bowl with the paddle attachment, beat butter and cream cheese until completely smooth, about 10 minutes. Turn mixer speed to low and add powdered sugar. Beat until smooth. Add vanilla and beat until light and creamy.

Lemon Cream Cheese

Instructions:

Add 3 tablespoons Lemon Cream (127) to a batch of Cream Cheese Icing (120). Beat until smooth.

Grapefruit Cream Cheese

Instructions:

Add the zest and juice of ½ grapefruit to a batch of Cream Cheese Icing (120). Beat until smooth. Add 1 cup powdered sugar if needed and beat until smooth.

Orange Cream Cheese

Instructions:

Add the zest and juice of one orange to a batch of Cream Cheese Icing (120). Add 1–2 cups powdered sugar to thicken and beat until smooth.

Peanut Butter Cream Cheese

Instructions:

Add 1 cup peanut butter to a batch of Cream Cheese Icing (120). Beat until smooth.

Honey Cream Cheese

Instructions:

Add 4 tablespoons honey to a batch of Cream Cheese Icing (120). Beat until smooth. Add 1 cup powdered sugar if needed and beat until smooth.

Coconut Cream Cheese

Instructions:

Add 2 teaspoons coconut extract and ¼ cup coconut milk to a batch of Cream Cheese Icing (120). Add 1–2 cups powdered sugar to thicken and beat until smooth.

Molasses Cream Cheese

4 oz. cream cheese, softened
2 Tbsp. butter, softened
2 Tbsp. molasses
2 cups powdered sugar
2 Tbsp. whole milk
1½ tsp. vanilla extract

Instructions:

In a large bowl, add cream cheese and butter. Beat together until incorporated and smooth. Add molasses and mix well. Mix in powdered sugar, milk, and vanilla, alternating ingredients as you mix until light and creamy.

German Chocolate Icing

1 cup evaporated milk
1 cup sugar
3 egg yolks
½ cup butter
2 tsp. vanilla extract
1½ cups chopped pecans
1½ cups shredded coconut

Instructions:

In a large saucepan over medium heat, combine evaporated milk, sugar, egg yolks, butter, and vanilla. Cook, stirring constantly, for 2–3 minutes. Turn heat to low and, still stirring constantly, cook until thick. Remove from heat and stir in pecans and coconut. Serve when just slightly warm.

Whipped Mascarpone Icing

8 oz. mascarpone cheese
1 cup powdered sugar
pinch of salt
1 tsp. vanilla
1½ cups heavy cream

Instructions:

Combine mascarpone cheese, powdered sugar, salt, and vanilla. Stir together until smooth and set aside.

Pour heavy cream into the bowl of an electric mixer and beat until stiff peaks form. Do not overmix. Fold whipped cream into the mascarpone mixture until combined. Use immediately.

Toppings & Fillings

Dark Chocolate Ganache

1 cup heavy cream
2 cups finely chopped good-quality
   bittersweet chocolate

Instructions:

Place chocolate in a large heatproof bowl. Bring cream to a simmer on stovetop until just before boiling, then pour mixture over chocolate. Let stand, without stirring, until the chocolate begins to melt.

Using a whisk, start at the center of the mixture and stir until the chocolate and cream are combined and smooth. Do not overmix.

Place a layer of plastic wrap directly on the ganache and refrigerate, stirring every 5 minutes until the mixture begins to cool and thicken.

Mint Chocolate Ganache

Instructions:

Using the recipe for Dark Chocolate Ganache (above), replace half of the chocolate with mint chocolate pieces.

White Chocolate Ganache

Instructions:

Using the recipe for Dark Chocolate Ganache (left), replace bittersweet chocolate with white chocolate.

Caramel Filling

½ cup butter
1 cup packed brown sugar
½ cup heavy cream

Instructions:

In a small saucepan, melt butter and stir in brown sugar and cream. Bring to a boil over medium to high heat for about 5 minutes. Reduce heat and simmer for 3–4 minutes or until caramel sauce begins to thicken.

Toasted Coconut

shredded coconut

Instructions:

Preheat oven to 350 degrees. Spread coconut evenly on baking sheet lined with parchment paper. Toast coconut, stirring occasionally, until it begins to brown, about 8–10 minutes. Cool completely before using.

Lime Curd

¾ cup egg yolks
¾ cup whole eggs
¾ cup sugar
¾ cup fresh lime juice
zest of 4 limes
¾ cup unsalted butter, softened

Instructions:

Mix the egg yolks, eggs, sugar, and lime juice together. Add the lime zest and butter. Cook in a double boiler until thickened. Check the temperature with a candy thermometer, making sure it reaches 160 degrees. Strain the mixture and then mix with a whisk until smooth. Refrigerate until needed. Mixture should be completely cool before using.

NOTE: Do not skip the straining process! This will catch the unwanted zest and overcooked eggs, resulting in a smooth and tangy lime curd.

Lemon Cream

¾ cup egg yolks
¾ cup whole eggs
¾ cup sugar
¾ cup fresh lemon juice
zest of 4 lemons
¾ cup unsalted butter, softened

Instructions:

Mix the egg yolks, eggs, sugar, and lemon juice together. Add the lemon zest and butter. Cook in a double boiler until thickened. Check the temperature with a candy thermometer, making sure it reaches 160 degrees. Strain the mixture and then mix with a whisk until smooth. Refrigerate until needed. Mixture should be completely cool before using.

NOTE: Do not skip the straining process! This will catch the unwanted zest and overcooked eggs, resulting in a smooth, delicious lemon cream.

Berry Puree
(Raspberry, Strawberry, or Blackberry)

1½ cups fresh or frozen berries
¼ cup sugar
2 Tbsp. lemon juice

Instructions:

Combine berries, sugar, and lemon juice in a saucepan and cook over medium heat, stirring occasionally, until a liquid begins to form. Continue cooking until the mixture starts to thicken. Pour sauce into a fine sieve set over a bowl. Use a rubber spatula to stir and press the puree through the sieve; throw the seeds away. Refrigerate. May be frozen for up to 1 month. Yields approximately 1 cup puree.

Mango Puree

2 ripe mangoes
2 Tbsp. water
¼ cup sugar

Instructions:

Peel, pit, and slice mangoes into chunks. Add water, sugar, and mangoes to a blender and blend until smooth. Yields 3 cups.

Streusel Topping

1 cup flour
1 cup oatmeal
1 cup packed brown sugar
2¼ tsp. ground cinnamon
¼ tsp. salt
¾ cup unsalted butter, softened

Instructions:

Mix together flour, oatmeal, brown sugar, cinnamon, and salt. Cut in the butter with your fingers until combined but still crumbly.

Peanut Butter Filling

4 Tbsp. unsalted butter, softened
¾ cup smooth, creamy peanut butter
½ cup powdered sugar
¼ tsp. salt
½ tsp. vanilla

Instructions:

Place all ingredients in the bowl of a stand mixer and mix on medium speed until smooth and creamy.

Easy Decorating Ideas

Marshmallow Fondant

ingredients

16 oz. mini marshmallows

4 Tbsp. water (adjust as needed, depending on climate)

2 lbs. powdered sugar

½ cup shortening

Preparation

1. *Put marshmallows* and 4 tablespoons water in a large microwave-safe bowl.

2. *Place in* microwave for 30 seconds, stir, and repeat until marshmallows are completely melted.

3. *Add 1½* pounds powdered sugar (start with 1½ pounds and add more as needed, up to 2 pounds). Begin stirring powdered sugar into marshmallows until the dough becomes thick and difficult to stir.

4. *Generously spread* shortening onto the top of the counter and pour marshmallow and sugar mixture on top.

5. *Coat your* hands or gloves with shortening and begin kneading the mixture until all of the powdered sugar is incorporated and it has become a soft pliable dough. If the fondant seems too dry and is tearing easily, add ½ tablespoon of water and knead until the dough becomes a smooth elastic ball and will stretch without tearing.

NOTE: To store the fondant, knead into a tight ball and double-wrap with plastic wrap. The fondant will store in the refrigerator for 3 weeks.

Janell Brown

Dinosaur Cupcakes

tools

Marshmallow Fondant (132)*

3 different gel food colorings

X-Acto knife

toothpicks

edible-ink marker

Vanilla Buttercream (118),
colored blue

offset spatula

powdered sugar

pizza cutter

small paintbrush

water

Vanilla Buttercream (118),
colored green

pastry bag

grass tip, Wilton #233

*Divide the fondant into fourths and color three sections using gel food colors. Leave the fourth section white.

Elasmosaurus

directions

1. *Select one color.* Roll a small ball of fondant, about the diameter of a quarter, into a smooth ball. Then begin to shape into a long hot dog shape.

2. *Using the X-Acto* knife, cut one end of the hot dog shape to the desired length of your dinosaur's neck.

3. *Using your fingers,* bend the rounded end of the neck down to form a head. Cut a small mouth with the X-Acto knife.

4. *Insert a toothpick* into the bottom of the neck.

5. *Using an edible-ink* marker, create two eyes on either side of the head.

6. *Take the other* end of the hot dog shape and roll the uncut tip to a slight point. Curl the end upward to create the dinosaur's tail.

7. *Insert a toothpick* and allow pieces to dry for at least one hour.

8. *Ice the top* of cupcake with blue buttercream with an offset spatula to create waves.

9. *Place the head* and tail of the dinosaur into the cupcake.

Stegosaurus

directions

1. *Dust countertop lightly* with powdered sugar and roll fondant to ¼-inch thick.

2. *Using X-Acto knife,* cut out a half circle to create the shape of your dinosaur.

3. *Roll out a* second color of fondant to ¼-inch thick.

4. *Using the pizza* cutter, cut a small rectangle of the second color. Cut small triangles with X-Acto knife.

5. *Using the paintbrush* and a small amount of water, attach triangles, point up, along the spine of the dinosaur.

6. *Use the edible-ink* marker to create eyes.

7. *Ice the top* of cupcake with green buttercream in the pastry bag fitted with the grass tip.

8. *Allow dinosaur* to dry at least 1 hour and place on top of cupcake.

T-Rex

directions

1. *Take the last* color of fondant and divide into sections. Roll a quarter-sized ball for the body. Taper one end to create the neck.

2. *Roll a nickel-sized* ball for the head. Shape into an oval. Roll two small tapered ovals for the arms.

3. *Dust countertop with* a light coat of powdered sugar. Roll out white fondant. Using the pizza cutter, cut a small rectangle for the mouth of the T-Rex. Use a toothpick to create teeth marks on the fondant.

4. *Place a toothpick* in the body of the T-Rex. Use the paintbrush and a small amount of water to attach the head, arms, and mouth.

5. *Roll out more* of the colored fondant to ¼-inch thick and cut a small rectangle. Use the X-Acto knife to make 3 triangles for the spikes on the head. Use water and paintbrush to attach.

6. *Draw eyes with* the edible-ink marker. Allow to dry for at least one hour.

7. *Ice the top* of cupcake with grass tip and place T-Rex on top.

Ballerina Cupcakes

tools

1 recipe Vanilla
Buttercream (118)

pink gel food coloring

spatula

pastry bag

large rose tip,
Wilton #125

powdered sugar

marshmallow fondant (132),
tinted light pink

Wilton shirt cutter

X-Acto knife

water

small paintbrush

pearl dragées

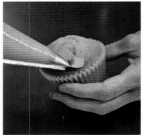

Dress

directions

1. *Separate buttercream into* three separate bowls. Color one bowl's buttercream to the darkest shade of pink (other colors may be used). Stir with a spatula until the color is completely incorporated. Take one scoop of the colored icing and place it into a bowl of plain buttercream. Stir until incorporated. Take one scoop of icing from this bowl and place it into the last bowl of plain buttercream. Stir until incorporated. You now have three shades of icing to complete the skirt.

2. *Cut a small* opening in a pastry bag and drop rose tip inside, making sure the tip is exposed. Fill the bag half full with colored buttercream. Twist the top of the bag closed, and hold firmly with your piping

138

hand. Make sure the thin part of the rose tip is pointing away from you. Hold the bag at a 45-degree angle. While applying even pressure, squeeze the bag and move the tip forward and back to create a petal.

3. *Turn the cupcake* counterclockwise and form the next petal. Complete one row of petals and then start a second row just above the first.

4. *Apply two rows* of each color until you reach the center of the cupcake.

 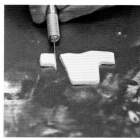  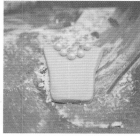

Top

directions

1. *Dust countertop with* a light layer of powdered sugar and roll out a small amount of light pink fondant to ¼-inch thick.

2. *Using the shirt* cutter from Wilton's people cutter set, cut out the number of shirts needed for your cupcakes.

3. *Using the X-Acto* knife, cut the arms off the shirt at a slight angle.

4. *Using the bottom* side of an icing tip, cut the neckline of the shirt.

5. *Apply a small* amount of water along the neckline with paintbrush and place pearl dragées in a row to create a necklace.

6. *Allow the shirts* to dry for at least one hour, then place in the center of cupcakes.

Christmas Wreath Cupcakes

Cupcakes

directions

1. *Ice tops of* 9 cupcakes with a thin layer of vanilla buttercream.

2. *Fit pastry bag* with leaf tip and fill with green buttercream.

3. *Holding the bag* at a 45-degree angle, squeeze, pull back, and release to create a leaf on cupcake.

4. *Starting on one* side of the cupcake, create a line of leaves. Move up and repeat the line of leaves, slightly overlapping the first row. Continue until the top of the cupcake is completely covered. Repeat for all 9 cupcakes.

5. *Place cupcakes in* a circle with the piped leaves facing the same way to create a wreath.

141

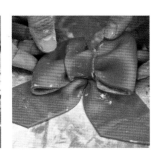

Bow

directions

1. *Dust countertop* lightly with powdered sugar and roll red fondant to ⅛-inch thick.

2. *Using a pizza* cutter, cut a medium-sized rectangle.

3. *Fold one side* of the rectangle to the middle, and repeat on the opposite side.

4. *Pinch the folded* rectangle together with both hands and begin to press them together, creating a bow.

5. *Cut a small* rectangle from fondant and lay over the center of the bow to create a knot.

6. *Cut two more* rectangles from fondant and cut ends at an angle to create the appearance of ribbon. Press the top of the rectangle together to make the fondant pucker.

7. *Place the bow* on the bottom cupcake in the cupcake wreath.

8. *Roll small balls* of red fondant to create berries and place on wreath.

Easy Wedding Cupcakes

tools

Vanilla Buttercream (118),
various colors

pastry bags

large star tip,
Ateco #829

pearl dragées

small rose tip,
Wilton #104

large rose tip,
Wilton #125

Swirls and Pearls

directions

1. *Ice top of* cupcake using tinted buttercream and pastry bag fitted with star tip.

2. *Sprinkle pearl dragées* on top.

Ruffles

directions

1. *Fit a pastry* bag with rose tip and fill with buttercream

2. *Hold the bag* at a 45-degree angle with the large end of the rose tip pointing down.

3. *Using a zigzag* motion, begin squeezing the icing, moving it along one side of cupcake.

4. *Repeat this motion,* moving up cupcake until the top is completely covered.

Flowers and Pearls

directions

1. *Fit a pastry* bag with rose tip and fill with tinted buttercream.

2. *Make sure the* thin part of the rose tip is pointing away from you.

3. *Hold the bag* at a 45-degree angle and, while squeezing, move the tip up, over, and down the top of cupcake to create a large petal.

4. *Turn the cupcake* counterclockwise and form the next petal. Complete the first row of petals and start a smaller second row just above the first.

5. *Finish the flower* by adding a center of pearl dragées.

NOTE: These cupcakes can be iced in a variety of colors and flowers. By using a medium star tip, hydrangeas can be created, and a leaf tip will produce succulents!

Covered in Pearls

directions

1. *Ice the top* of cupcake with a thin layer of buttercream.

2. *Fill a small* bowl with pearl dragées.

3. *Roll the top* of cupcake in dragées until the top is completely covered.

Petal Pleats

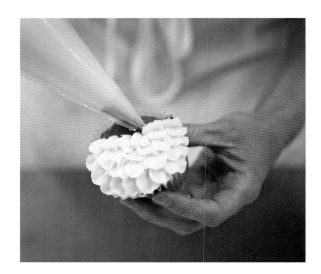

directions

1. *Fit a pastry* bag with large rose tip and fill with buttercream.

2. *Holding the bag* at a 45-degree angle, start on one side of cupcake and, while squeezing, move the bag up, over, and down to create a small petal.

3. *Repeat this motion,* creating a line across the top of cupcake. Move up cupcake and create another line of petals that slightly overlap the first.

4. *At the end* of cupcake, pipe a straight line of icing from top to bottom and embellish with pearls.

Firecracker Popsicle Cupcakes

tools

red, white, and blue–tinted marshmallow fondant (132)

rolling pin

X-Acto knife

toothpicks

Vanilla Buttercream (118)

directions

1. *Roll red, white,* and blue fondant to ¼-inch thick.

2. *Cut three rectangles* the same size of each color and lay together in order of red at the top, white in the middle, and blue on the bottom.

3. *Lightly roll over* all three colors with the rolling pin.

4. *Use the X-Acto* knife, cut out the shape of a popsicle.

5. *Insert a toothpick* in the bottom of the popsicle.

6. *Roll the blue* fondant to ¼-inch thick and cut out the shape of popsicle drips. These do not need to be exact or all look the same.

7. *Ice the top* of cupcake with buttercream and top with popsicle drips and then popsicles.

Spring Flowers Cupcakes

tools

Chocolate Buttercream (118)

crushed Oreos

pastry bags

Vanilla Buttercream (118),
4 different colors

small rose tip,
Wilton #104

small star tip,
Wilton #16

leaf tip, Wilton #352

directions

1. *Ice the top* of cupcake with a small layer of chocolate buttercream. Dip the top in crushed Oreos.

2. *Fit pastry bags* with tips and fill with colored buttercream.

3. *Use rose tip* to create a 5-petal flower by holding the bag at a 45-degree angle and, while squeezing, move the bag up, over, and down to create a petal. Rotate cupcake until the flower is complete.

4. *Using star tip,* hold pastry bag at a 90-degree angle and, while squeezing, move bag clockwise to create a small rosette.

5. *Using star tip,* squeeze and release small stars in a circle to create groups of hydrangeas.

6. *Using the leaf* tip, fill in empty spaces with leaves.

Janell Brown

Baby Shower Cupcakes

tools

Vanilla Buttercream (118)

rock sugar

3 zip-top bags

food color gels

powdered sugar

marshmallow fondant (132)

large tip
(or circle cutter)

toothpicks

small round tip,
Wilton #3

pastry bag

Vanilla Buttercream (118)

directions

1. *Ice the top* of cupcakes with tinted vanilla buttercream.

2. *Divide rock sugar* and place into 3 separate bags. Add 3 drops of color to the first bag, one drop to the second, and ¼ drop to the third.

3. *Seal the bag* and begin to rub the sugar and color together until the sugar is completely coated with the desired color. Repeat with the other two bags and pour rock sugar into three separate bowls.

4. *Press and roll* iced cupcakes into rock sugar to completely cover the top of cupcake.

5. *Dust countertop with* powdered sugar and roll fondant to ¼-inch thick. Using the bottom side of the large tip, cut out circles and place a toothpick in the bottom of each one.

6. *Using the top* of the small tip, create a border around the circles by gently pressing the top of the tip into the fondant.

7. *Fit pastry bag* with tip #3 and fill with vanilla buttercream. Write one letter on each fondant disc and place in cupcakes.

8. *Display cupcakes together* to create the message you want to send.

Perfect Pumpkins

orange-tinted fondant (132)

toothpicks

brown-tinted fondant (132)

paintbrush

water

directions

1. *Roll a quarter-sized* ball with orange fondant until smooth.

2. *Press the center* of ball to flatten slightly.

3. *Use a toothpick* to create lines around the ball to form the shape of a pumpkin.

4. *Roll a small* piece of brown fondant to look like a pumpkin stem.

5. *Using the paintbrush,* apply a small amount of water to the top of the pumpkin and attach the stem.

6. *Allow to dry* for at least 1 hour and then place on top of iced cupcakes.

Index

Index

Index

About the Author

Janell Brown joined the cupcake industry when, faced with financial struggles, she decided to take her hobby to the next level. In her adventure, she has turned a fun stay-at-home-mom craft into a successful business. Her story is one of hard work, determination, challenges, and success. In 2012 she won *Cupcake Wars* on Food Network, which launched her business to new levels. Janell resides in West Jordan, Utah, with her husband and four children.

You can see more of her work at
www.OneSweetSlice.com.